THE MIDDLE EAST AND PROBLEMS OF DEMOCRACY

ISSUES IN THIRD WORLD POLITICS

Series Editor: Vicky Randall, Department of Government, University of Essex.

Current titles:
Heather Deegan: The Middle East and problems of democracy
Jeff Haynes: Religion in Third World politics
Robert Pinkney: Democracy in the Third World

THE MIDDLE EAST AND PROBLEMS OF DEMOCRACY

Heather Deegan

LYNNE RIENNER PUBLISHERS
Boulder, Colorado

Published in the United States of America in 1994 by
Lynne Rienner Publishers, Inc.
1800 30th Street, Boulder, Colorado

© 1994 by Heather Deegan. All rights reserved

Library of Congress Cataloging-in-Publication Data
Deegan, Heather.
The Middle East and problems of democracy / Heather Deegan.
p. cm. – (Issues in Third World politics)
Includes bibliographical references and index.
ISBN 1-55587-455-X (alk. paper)
1. Middle East – Politics and government – 1979- 2. Democracy – Middle East. I. Title. II. Series.
JQ1758.A91D43 1993
320.956—dc20 93-4446
CIP

Printed and bound in Great Britain

320.956
D31

94-0227
28148886

Contents

Series editor's introduction

When I was invited to edit this series, I thought long and hard about what it should be called. I ended up going back to the well-worn phrase 'Third World' but recognizing that this very term raises problems that both this Introduction and the books in the series would need to address. Its advantage is that to most people it signals something fairly clearcut and recognizable. The expression 'Third World' has come to connote the regions and individual countries of Africa, Asia, the Caribbean, Latin America and the Middle East. It is the politics, in the broadest sense, of this part of the world, and of its relationship with the rest of the world, that constitutes the subject matter of this series.

Yet the notion of a single 'Third World' has always been problematic. When it became clear that the nations so designated were not going to follow a third, 'nonaligned', economic and political route between the capitalist west and the communist world, it was argued that they none the less shared a common predicament. Directly or indirectly they suffered the after-effects of colonization and they came late and on disadvantageous terms into the competitive world economy. Even then there was tremendous variety – in culture, experience of colonial rule, forms and levels of economic activity – between and within Third World regions.

Over time this internal differentiation seems to have grown. On the one hand we have the oil-rich states and the Newly Industrializing Countries (NICs), on the other the World Bank has identified a 'Fourth World' of lower income countries like Bangladesh or Tanzania, distinguished from the lower-middle income countries like Mexico and Malaysia. Then from the later 1980s we have witnessed the disintegration of most of the 'Second World' of state socialist societies – where does that leave the First and the Third?

These developments certainly threaten the coherence of the concept of a Third World. They must make us wonder whether the concept is any longer plausible or useful in categorizing what are by now well over 100 countries, containing three-quarters of the world's population. Recently writers both on the right and on the left have suggested that the notion of a Third World functions primarily as a myth: for the former it is a projection of the guilt of First World liberals while for the latter it evokes for the West a reassuring image of its own opposite, all that it has succeeded in not becoming.

The arguments are not all one way, however. When Nigel Harris writes about the 'end of the Third World' and its dissolution into one world economic system, he is referring to objective economic trends which still have a long way to go and which are by no means automatically accompanied by a decline in western economic nationalism or cultural chauvinism. Third World countries do still at least some of the time recognize their common status *vis-à-vis* the developed world and the need to stick together, as was apparent at the Rio Earth Summit in June 1992. The fact that some Third World nations may have 'made it' into the developed world, does not negate the existence of the Third World they have left behind. It does, however, undermine the more deterministic arguments of dependency theorists, who have maintained that it is impossible to break out of economic dependence and underdevelopment. The dissolution of the Second World, it could be argued, leaves the confrontation and contrast between First and Third World starker than ever (this might of course indicate the use of a different nomenclature, such as North and South). On the other hand the countries of the old Second World will not be transformed overnight into members of the First and there is a case for retaining a Second World category to refer to countries only recently emerged from a prolonged period of communist rule.

But my purpose here is not to insist on the continuing usefulness of the notion of a Third World so much as to signal the question as part of the agenda I hope that authors in this series will address. It seems to me that there *are* respects in which most of the countries conventionally included in the Third World do continue to share a common predicament and about which it is up to a point legitimate to generalize. But unless we also explore the differences between them, our powers of political explanation will be limited and it may be that it is these differences which now hold answers to the most important and interesting questions we want to ask.

Perhaps the key political issue in contemporary Third World studies is democratization. Yet, as Heather Deegan points out, when it comes to the Middle East, the widespread assumption seems to be that there is little to say about democracy and most of it negative. Such a peremptory dismissal is unwarranted. The questions of democracy and democratization in the Middle East deserve closer attention. Enriching her argument with a series of country-based Middle Eastern case studies, she shows how a more detailed examination can reveal both the relevance and also the limitations of current western theorizing about the meaning and prospects of democracy in the Third World.

Vicky Randall

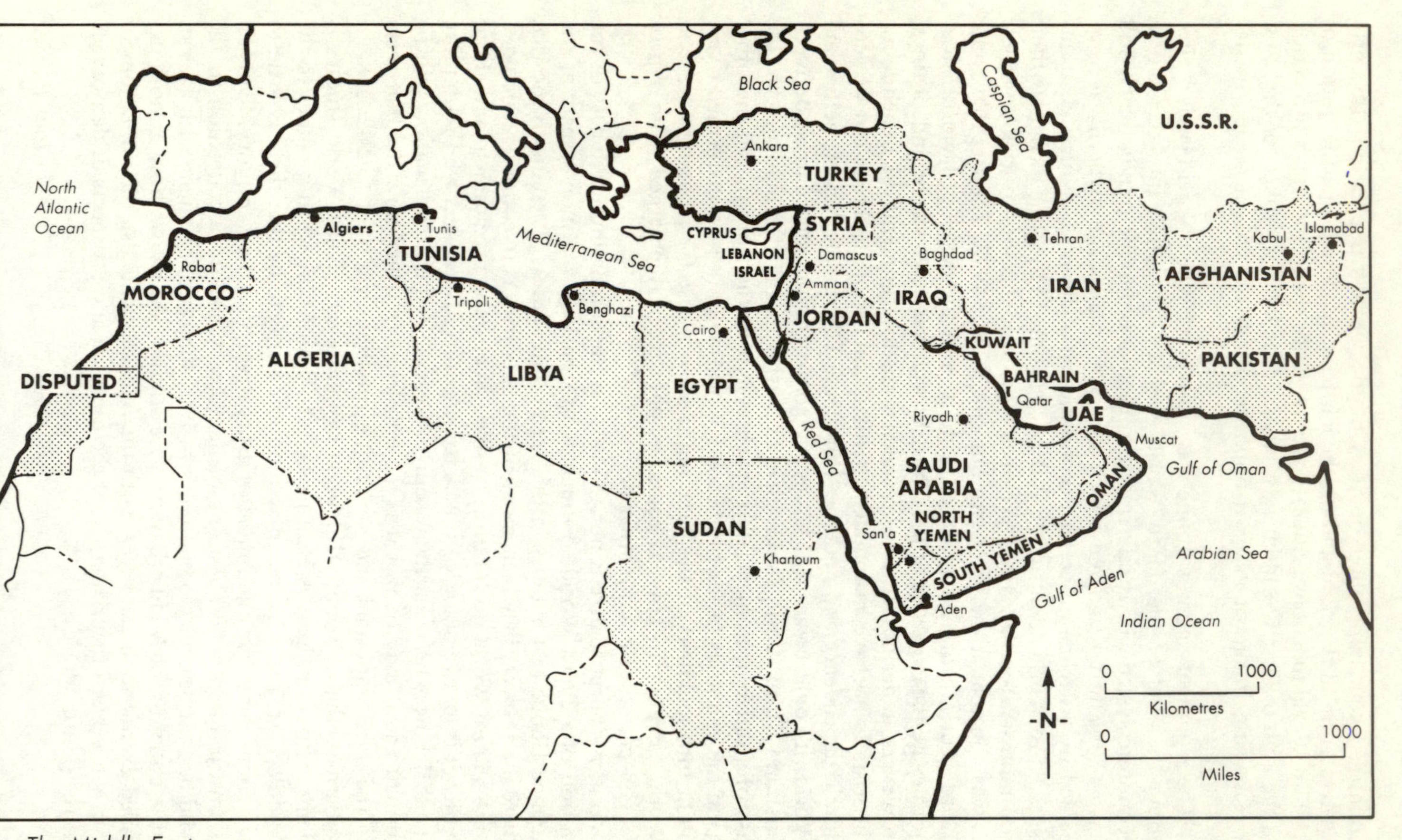

The Middle East

Democracy and democratization

> The pure idea of democracy, according to its definition, is the government of the whole people by the whole people, equally represented.[1]

> [Democracy means] only that the people have the opportunity of accepting or refusing the men who are to rule them.[2]

> Classic assumptions about the need for citizen participation in democracy were inadequate. What we call 'democracy' seems to operate with a relatively low level of citizen participation.[3]

If the search for democracy in the Middle East is not to be equated with the quest for eternal life there must exist some basic understanding of precisely what the term implies and more importantly, what it demands of both population and political system. Yet, perversely, democracy is not so easily defined and tends to divide sharply between normative and empirical accounts. Normative theory stresses the vision of a 'good' society which rests on assumptions of human capabilities and potentialities. Empirical theory, on the other hand, is based on a set of concepts and classifications used in describing and explaining political reality as it exists in the modern world.

Although the term democracy is now used as a statement of commendation, in its classical mode it was vague, the 'power of people' or 'will of people' are open to various interpretations as is the view that democracy necessarily assumes a population's tacit consent to its government. In the writings of the nineteenth-century theorist John Stuart Mill, democracy was inextricably linked with representative government, which in order to exist at all had to meet three fundamental conditions: 'People should be willing to receive it; they should be willing and able to do what is necessary for its preservation; and they should be willing and able to fulfil the duties and discharge the functions which it imposes on them.'[4] For Mill the participation of a country's citizenry in communal activities and, specifically political affairs, was crucial to the development of representative government. To be denied active participation and be consigned to a life of passivity created a sadly impoverished people deprived of intellectual stimulus and lacking 'any potential voice in their own destiny'.[5] Participation through the ballot box would be self-improving, would reveal the general interest of the community at large and would render society more cohesive, in that powerful groups would be absorbed into society, thus reducing the need for recourse to violence and disorder. Voting would provide the key to participation but it was not simply to be a carefree act of indulgence, the voter was under an absolute 'moral obligation to consider the interests of the public, not his private advantage and to give his vote to the best of his judgement'.[6]

It was a curious feature that a man hailed as a democratic theorist and so committed to the franchise should, in later years, be criticized as undemocratic on the grounds of its prescribed limitations. From the vantage point of nineteenth-century Britain, Mill advocated the extension of the franchise, but not immediately. Rather it should be introduced at some point in the future, 'when a general degree of the community will allow'.[7] Enfranchisement, then, was to be a limited affair in the short term, confined to those of superior mental ability; a quality which could be divined through the assessment of a person's occupation. Thus, a foreman would be more intelligent than a labourer; an employer more so than an employee; a banker more so than a tradesman, and so on.[8] Achieving universal suffrage, although undoubtedly a desirable goal should remain a gradual process. In classical democratic theory, voting or indeed political action as a whole, had to be informed, impartial, thoughtful and self-improving.

It should come as no surprise, however, that when sociologists and political scientists investigated voting behaviour in the United States during the 1950s they discovered that a significant proportion of the electorate were either politically ignorant or indifferent, or both. In Berelson's opinion: 'If the democratic system depended solely on the qualifications of the individual voter it seems remarkable that democracies have survived through the centuries.'[9] Societies which called themselves democracies revealed a high degree of apathy among the electorate and this led to the formation of a revisionist school of thought known as 'new Democratic Theory', which cast aspersions on classical theories of participation. Empirical studies of voting trends clashed with normative political theory with the result that defining democracy became more difficult.[10] If enfranchised people actually failed to vote in stable democratic countries in the second half of the twentieth century then this actuality sharply confronted theoretical assumptions about the efficacy of participation in a democracy. In short 'what is' was juxtaposed with 'what should be' and a whole body of literature was devoted to examining the disparities. As the classical supposition of a uniquely well-informed and interested electorate fully participating in the political process could not be replicated empirically, electoral apathy came to be seen as essential in maintaining stability. Mass participation was associated with societal disorder and a tendency towards totalitarianism, with echoes of a fascist or communist state. The democratic function was to be embraced in the notion of 'a competitive theory of democracy'. Joseph Schumpeter, one of its chief proponents, defined the method as 'that institutional arrangement for arriving at political decisions in which individuals acquire the power to decide by means of a competitive struggle for the people's vote'.[11] Thus, 'free competition for a free vote' became a fundamental condition of the democratic system. Where no effective competition existed, the system ceased to be one in which the leaders were responsive to the independent wishes of non-leaders.

The general model of this 'revisionist' competitive theory is that of groups competing at the top for the votes of a relatively apathetic majority during election periods.[12] The electorate is enabled to join in a process of selection or rejection of candidates who openly compete for public office. This system of pluralism is identified with liberalism and the acceptance of certain values, e.g. the rule of law which separates the legislative function from the executive one; the preservation of the liberties of the people: freedom of speech, freedom of association, freedom of press and freedom of assembly, which a government would be unable to violate; responsible government which is accountable to the people via elections; and the political equality of one person, one vote and equal sized constituencies. A pluralistic society represents competition between diverse groups but although diversity and opposition are stressed and groups are encouraged to disagree on particular issues there must exist an overriding commitment from all groups, to the rules of society. Should a group, party or organization, hold deeply antagonistic ideas about the functioning of the political system, it would be regarded as a threat to that society. Opposition, then, is the central feature of a liberal, pluralistic society but only so far as it seeks neither to undermine nor eliminate the structure of the state.

It is inevitable in a pluralist society for elites to form but these developments are defended on two grounds: first, elites exist because not everyone has political ability and second, the population can replace them at elections and, therefore, elites represent no threat. A pluralist democracy is realized if certain conditions are fulfilled, namely, if voters can choose between competing elites; elites do not have hereditary power; elites depend on the support of shifting coalitions and on whether different elites dominate in different spheres. Interest groups and pressure groups can exist within the system or outside it and are important in the influence they can exert over politicians.

Yet not all countries can avail themselves of pluralistic democracy for its development depends on a rigid set of conditions. Within the model of competitive theory truly democratic countries were considered to be those with a high standard of living and a reasonable spread of income which tended to diminish social unrest. Therefore, poverty, illiteracy, hunger and ignorance all served to render a country unlikely to sustain democracy, and with one sweep of analysis practically half the globe was condemned to undemocratic government.[13] Underdeveloped countries were seen to face enormous obstacles in that different religions, tribes and groups presented major difficulties in achieving national unity. Divisive and destructive forces would savage any attempts at unity and in the absence of a general toleration of varied opinions, opposition could not be institutionalized. Indeed, some parallels were drawn with early Western societies.

Democracy in the Third World

Since the 1950s there have been various theories and interpretations as to the political direction Third World countries should, would or, indeed, could contemplate. They largely fell into three distinctive categories: the Modernization School, the Dependency School and the Statist School, all of which are analysed in Randall and Theobalds *Political Change and Underdevelopment: A Critical Introduction to Third World Politics* (1985). It was perhaps inevitable that when confronted with the emergence of newly independent states, the early writings of political scientists should predict a process of political change which was both comparative and closely patterned on the Western model of political advancement.[14] Accordingly, a process of modernisation was identified against which a country's progression could be charted. This model assumed many guises but tended to coalesce around certain characteristics which had been factors in Western political development, namely: rationalization, national integration and nation building, democratization and participation. Whilst Dankwart Rustow defined political development as: 'Increasing national political unity plus a broadening base of political participation', Karl Deutsch viewed modernization as a complex process of social change which was 'significantly correlated with major changes in politics'.[15] Urbanization, improved literacy rates, expanding economies, exposure to mass communications were all factors which would combine to mobilize the population and increase demands for governmental services. Political participation was to be the key which opened the door to modern political development and thus distinguished the traditional society, which was non-participatory, separating people 'by kinship into communities isolated from each other and from a centre', from an advancing modernizing state.[16] A 'new world political culture', announced Almond and Verba in 1963, would be one of 'participation' and Frederick Frey suggested that the 'most common notion of political development is that of a movement towards democracy'.[17]

Yet it was not to be so straightforward. Lucien Pye, writing in 1964 raised a note of caution: 'The new states of the underdeveloped areas present us with a major challenge, for in a very fundamental sense the model that has emerged out of the tradition of empirical study of the American political process has been misleading when applied to most of the new states.'[18] Theories and models appropriate to the American system of government were of 'little relevance to many of the new countries'. There was clearly a need for a different approach which examined the elements at play in less developed countries and broached certain basic questions, e.g. 'To what extent was there a link between economic growth and national development? Was liberal-democracy too divisive for new nations and strong leadership under a single party more suitable? How was it possible to understand and interpret the drift towards authoritarian practice?' In short, as Pye put it: 'What should be taken as the criteria of political development?'[19]

These questions are, of course, yet to be resolved, but 25 years' ago, Samuel Huntington was critical of the presumed association between political advancement and socio-economic conditions. He maintained that such a linkage drastically constrained 'the applicability of the concept in both time and space', as the term political development became synonymous with a modern nation-state. It, therefore, became impossible to speak of a 'politically developed tribal authority, city-state, feudal monarchy or bureaucratic empire'.[20] Development was wrongly identified with one type of political system, and although obviously affected by the process of modernization, should essentially remain independent of it. Huntington defined the term as 'the institutionalisation of political organisations and procedures', and in so doing attempted to 'liberate development from modernisation'.[21]

According to one academic, the central difficulty with developing nations was the problems experienced as a result of a lack of integration. As societies progressed and conflicts began to multiply, procedures for the settlement of those conflicts were sometimes arbitrary and inappropriate. Consequently, such a system did little to appease the hostility of regions, tribes and religious groups who found themselves competing in a common political system. In the absence of integration, societies would be riven by 'parochial loyalties' which would undermine the political structure. Huntington seized on this view arguing that 'national disintegration' and 'national integration' were two sides of the same coin. If there was to be such a concept as political development, and it must be remembered that by 1971 Huntington had himself rejected the term in favour of 'political change', it had to embrace the notion of 'political decay' and the circumstances which brought it about.[22]

Political decay was a dispiriting notion but one which was becoming increasingly relevant as coups and violence beset newly developing countries. Huntington argued that in its early stages, economic development – precisely that factor which had been hailed as the harbinger of political potential and advancement – created dislocation in new nations with fragile political institutions. If governments failed to govern, 'political degeneration' would occur and any attempts to democratize would vanish in a haze of tyranny. Huntington looked to the writings of Kornhauser, published in 1957 for a depressing prognosis: 'Where the pre-established political authority is highly autocratic', stated Kornhauser in his study of mass society, 'rapid and violent displacement of that authority by a democratic regime is highly favourable to the emergence of extremist mass movements that tend to transform the new democracy in anti-democratic directions'.[23] Political stability and political order then, had to be maintained irrespective of the possible authoritarian implications. According to Randall and Theobalds, some writers found Huntington's views 'disturbing' in that 'the content of government – whether its policies were progressive – and the openness of government were of secondary importance.'[24]

Of course, it must be acknowledged that Huntington's latest writings support democratization but at that time as an authoritative academic, there were unquestionably undertones in his analysis especially when he turned his attention to the role which should be played by the United States. He counselled at the close of his essay on 'Political Development and Political Decay', that instead of relying on the military:

> American policy should be directed to the creation within modernising countries of at least one strong non-Communist political party. If such a party already exists and is in a dominant position, support of that party should be the keystone of policy. Where political life is fragmented and many small parties exist, American backing should go to the strongest of the parties whose goals are compatible with ours. If it is a choice between a party and a personality choose the party: better the Ba'ath Party than Nasser. Where no parties exist and the government (whether traditional, military, or charismatic) is reasonably cooperative with the United States, American military, economic and technical assistance should be conditioned upon the government's making efforts to develop a strong supporting party organisation.[25]

Huntington, however, liked to have his cake and eat it. Whilst he exhorted the United States to involve itself in the politics of independent states, when America did, often covertly through the apparatus of the Central Intelligence Agency (CIA), with attendant social and political costs, Huntington criticized the countries for their vulnerability, their lack of 'political autonomy' and the ease with which they were 'penetrated by agents, groups and ideas from other political systems'. In some instances, he proclaimed: 'a regime may be overthrown by smuggling into the country a few agents and a handful of weapons', at other times it only may take 'a few thousand dollars'.[26] As the political systems of numerous states drifted towards repression, in the form of military control and recurring coups d'état, the realization emerged that something had gone dreadfully wrong and academics began to re-orientate their thinking. The modernization political development argument became overshadowed by the dependency and underdevelopment approach: capitalist exploitation and imperialist ambition had largely stymied economic and political room for manoeuvre in the developing world. Attention turned to the Soviet model of development.

One analyst argued that it was readily recognized in post-colonial societies: 'a one-party or quasi-party system appears to be more appropriate than the competitive party model'.[27] This justification included an acceptance of Marxist-Leninist 'democratic centralist' ideas in that it assumed that in one-party states there existed a measure of democracy in the form of intra-party debate and inputs from interest groups within the organization. Also, as parties were judged to represent class interests, a one-party state could be accepted on the grounds of the existence of only one class in newly independent nations. A multi-party system was seen to be sectional and sterile with no true interest in the nation at heart. Therefore, underdeveloped countries needed to build up their political infrastructure and unite within a strongly centralized state which controlled both political institutions and economic activity. Although these regimes were regarded as being in a transition to democracy there existed no expectation that there would be any move towards a liberal democratic model in the foreseeable future. Indeed, it might even be considered presumptuous to consider there should be such a move.[28] In Macpherson's view democracy was only tangentially linked with liberalism and underdeveloped nations had 'rooted themselves in an earlier radical democratic tradition', which rejects competitive capitalist individualism in pursuit of 'moral worth, dignity and humanity', this form has apparently 'as good a claim to the title democracy as has the now more familiar pluralistic liberal democracy'.[29] The problem with liberal democracy was its emphasis on 'possessive individualism' and the assumption that society was little more than a series of market relations between individuals.[30]

A decade later other analysts found the linkage important: 'The process by which democracy was "liberalised" is a key one, for it ties together notions of capitalist development, class formation and class conflict, as well as such essentials of liberal democracy as competitive parties and majority rule.'[31] If liberal democracy is coterminous with *laissez-faire* economies it is precisely the nature of those economic conditions which underpin its stability. As Lipset pointed out in 1963 at the height of the modernization debate: 'Men may question whether any aspect of this interrelated cluster of economic development . . . gradual political change, legitimacy and democracy is primary, but the fact remains that the cluster does hang together.'[32] Liberal democracy, then, not only requires a supportive economic climate but also, it needs as a prerequisite some degree of social cohesion and political consensus.

So, after numerous models, theories, revisions and reappraisals of modes and methods of political change in the developing world, two questions emerge. First, why consider democracy at this precise time, and second, where exactly does the Middle East fit in the wider picture of Third World politics. Well, in answer to the first query, the renewed interest is obviously partly to do with what has been actually happening in the Third World in the context of moves towards democratization, in the form of the reintroduction of multi-party politics and a tentative shift towards pluralism. In the last few years there has been an obvious shift in the political climate of a number of developing states, indeed to such an extent that reports emerged of a new 'wind of change' blowing through Africa and other Third World nations. The Organization of African Unity spoke of the need to democratize the societies of member states and at a meeting of the Non-aligned Movement (NAM) in 1991 reference was made to the need to take seriously 'the expansion of liberalism' and the adoption of multi-party democracy.[33] This new trend in political pluralism at the expense of the one-party state was established in the wake of the dissolution of the Soviet Union and with the endorsement of the West, aid agencies, the International Monetary Fund and the World Bank. Inevitably, these political changes have aroused academic enquiry and comment on the efficacy of pluralist, multi-party systems of government in the Third World and have renewed the debate about the essential conditions of democracy and indeed, its suitability and sustainability.[34]

However, the Middle East has been generally left out of the debate. The second question, then, demands more attention chiefly because there has been very little discussion of democratization in the Third World which actually includes the Middle East. In the study by Diamond et al., of 26 countries in Latin America, Africa and Asia, the states of the Middle East, Islamic and otherwise were omitted, on the grounds that 'they generally lack much previous democratic experience, and most appear to have little prospect of transition even to semi-democracy'.[35] Similarly, though from a Marxist perspective, Giacomo Luciani writing in the 1980s of the notion of the 'rentier state' also implied that democratization in the Middle East was unviable. The 'rentier state' analysis, which will be considered again in further chapters, rests on the hypothesis that external sources of income resulting from the export of oil, in other words, oil revenue, is in fact a form of rent. Income is raised by the state, not through the more traditional route of domestic taxation and economic strategy, which are often seen to be associated with popular demands for political reform and legitimacy, but externally through the commodity of oil. In a sense, the economic development argument is turned on its head because although many Middle Eastern states are vastly wealthy in terms of gross national product which might present a prima facie case for political development, the nature of the wealth is not the result of industrialization and societal differentiation, factors once seen as necessary to political change, but simply the result of enormous oil revenues. As Luciani states: 'The need to raise revenue is the basic reason why the state has an interest in the prosperity and economic well-being of its country.' Without such an interest, it is inevitable that 'rentier states will display little tendency to evolve towards democratic institutions'.[36]

Certainly, then, there has tended to be a feeling that the Middle East is something of a 'lost cause'; a view which largely rests on the assumption that 'tremendous barriers' exist to the establishment of 'fully-functioning democratic political systems' in the region.[37] Curiously, all those politically debilitating features delineated so comprehensively in the early literature on political development are still judged to be characteristics of the region:

weak institutionally; divided ethnically; tethered to authoritarian structures of government; lacking in unity, political legitimacy and tolerance of opposition; exploited by the external factor of the Cold War and recently, in thrall to fundamentalist religion, the countries of the Middle East have been regarded as possessing elements inimical to any form of democratization.

This study, however, disagrees with this view and intends to argue a number of points which will be raised at this stage but will be further elaborated in subsequent chapters. First, the situation in the Middle East is changing, particularly after the 1991 Gulf War, and the implication of these changes for democracy should be discussed. Second, in this discussion the notion of democracy should not solely be confined to liberal democracy. Third, and on the other hand, some of the new developments, for example in terms of the re-introduction of elections, the removal of bans on political parties and more generally in the sphere of participation, may be viewed as steps paving the way for fuller democratization in a liberal democratic sense. Certainly, there has been considerable discussion of democracy in the Middle East recently particularly from what previously might have been regarded as unlikely quarters. President Assad of Syria announced at a ceremony in March 1992 marking his new seven-year term of office: 'Democracy does not mean political chaos. It means making available the best circumstances that enable the citizen to make a free choice.'[38] A few months earlier King Hussein of Jordan declared in favour of 'democratization and political pluralism', with due care and attention to be paid to freedom of expression and human rights.[39] The Lebanese Prime Minister proclaimed the government's commitment to 'parliamentary and municipal elections, held within a framework of freedom', and the Iraqi oppositionist group, the Supreme Assembly of the Islamic Revolution in Iraq (SAIRI) has reiterated its respect for 'freedom of opinion, the multi-party system and free elections'.[40] These developments in the political arena are beginning to attract attention from some academics, such as Michael Hudson, J. Esposito and James Piscatori.[41]

Yet it would be unwise to view the region as politically homogeneous. Distinct differences exist between the nation-states to the extent that a move towards democratization in one country may be symbolized by the removal of the ban on the formation of political parties, whilst in another, it might be characterized by the establishment of a more equitable parliamentary system. In other words, the political systems of say, Kuwait and Lebanon are so completely dissimilar they do not seem to brook comparison, yet the commonalities shared by their 'Arabness' are important factors in understanding political reform. In discussing democracy in the Middle East, then, one needs to recognize the significance of a number of particular constraints: population mobility, the question of refugees, immigration and their implication for citizenship; communal division and the possibilities and limitations of the consociational model of political organization; the role of Islam and until recently the Cold War. These aspects need to be introduced briefly here as they will reappear in subsequent chapters.

Population mobility and citizenship

Over a decade ago the Dutch academic, Herman van Gunsteren, lamented the demise of the concept of citizenship which he claimed had 'gone out of fashion among political thinkers'.[42] Today the concept is very much in intellectual fashion and in any analysis of democratization processes within Middle Eastern countries the role of citizenship is absolutely crucial. Indeed, in liberal democratic theory with its emphasis on the place of the individual's rights and responsibilities set within a legal framework, the citizen must assume a primary position.

Citizenship clearly constitutes the most basic conduit for integration into the state and defines a person's relationship with the political environment.[43] Van Gunsteren, however, sees the 'notions and practices of citizenship' to be 'variable and conflicting' containing ambiguities which truly reveal the 'conflicts and problems between a plurality of people whom history has brought together in relations of interdependence and dominance'.[44] Citizenship, then, is an area of 'contestation and struggle' centred on the inclusion or exclusion of persons within a nation-state. Historically, of course, there always existed certain qualifying conditions associated with citizenship, e.g.: gender, residence, property/land ownership, and so on, and this still remains the case. Citizenship implies the bestowal of certain rights and duties upon the individual and as such the good citizen will acknowledge and abide by the conventions and expectations of his or her society. Accordingly, there must be a procedure by which 'citizens exert control over government and make it aware of their demands, but correspondingly, there must also be a readiness to allow the government to enforce policies'.[45]

In other words, citizens are enfranchised and may participate in the political process but equally are under a duty to accept being ruled; otherwise there might be a drift towards mass politics, characterized by unruly large-scale activities of the citizenry outside the structure and rules instituted by society to govern political action. Mass politics is to be avoided at all costs for it involves violence against opposition; a lack of respect for minorities; the rejection of peaceful solutions to conflicts; the pursuit of short-term objectives and results in either anarchy or dictatorship.[46] The only way to counter this development is through the establishment of a pluralistic social structure which will enable the citizenry to form independent and limited pressure groups and facilitate the 'free and open competition for leadership, widespread participation in the selection of leaders and restraint in the application of pressures on leaders'.[47]

The role of citizenry, then, can be both stable and responsible given certain circumstances, but what is the situation in a region which witnesses a high degree of population mobility, for either political or economic reasons? The Arab states, particularly Lebanon, Syria, Jordan, Egypt and Kuwait utilize two basic principles in their definition of citizenship: *jus sanguinis* and *jus soli*. The principle of *jus sanguinis* recognizes an individual's citizenship as determined by the citizenship of his/her parents. *Jus soli*, on the other hand, holds that citizenship is based on the individual's place of birth. These two principles constitute the framework of Arab citizenship laws.[48] Citizenship carries political rights which vary depending on which country is under examination, but in a nation with a high degree of population mobility, naturalization processes become significant. Bahrain, Egypt, Iraq, Jordan, Kuwait, Syria and the United Arab Emirates all have naturalization laws which stipulate conditions such as the length of residency along with an individual's personal characteristics which must be fulfilled in order to become a naturalized citizen of a given state. In Kuwait, for example, with a population estimated to be in the region of 2.2 million on 1 August 1990, of which approximately 70 per cent was non-Kuwaiti, the question of citizenry and naturalization raises other important issues: the extent to which democratization can take place in a country in which nationals represent only 30 per cent of the population.[49] The residency requirement in Kuwait is between ten and thirty years before an applicant can apply for naturalization and then there is no guarantee that it will be granted. The decision to control naturalization procedures in what seems to be an exceptionally draconian way, together with the institution of restrictions on the rights of naturalized citizens, must be viewed against a background of spiralling immigration and newly acquired independence in the 1960s.[50] A large amorphous population was clearly at odds with the preservation of a nation-state identity; therefore, political rights were strictly controlled. Whilst naturalized Kuwaitis are granted citizenship rights such as civil service employment, property ownership and access to welfare benefits in the form of educational and retirement allowances they are not permitted the 'right to vote for any representative body until twenty years after the acquisition of citizenship and are ineligible for nomination or appointment to a representative body or ministerial position'.[51] It is quite apparent that within a given set of procedures citizenship can be graduated and controlled. In fact, it is the usual practice for countries to engage in this form of exercise but in nations in which the majority of the population falls into the non-citizen or semi-citizen categories democratization poses difficulties, in that participation can only be confined to the minority.

The lessons from history suggest that only when the issue of citizenship is approached can the questions of participation and democratization be fully embraced. According to S. S. Russell, 'States differ in the extent to which naturalisation has been used as a means to involve immigrants in the process of solidifying their own sense of identity as a state.'[52] The corollary of this statement is the assumption that nation-statehood demands a loyal citizenry enjoined with that particular state, and no other. The demands on the citizen are absolute. This concept is not just the subject of abstract discourse when applied to the position of the Palestinians and, more especially, their role within Jordan.

The displacement of the Palestinians during the 1948/1949 Arab-Israeli War; Jordan's subsequent annexation of the West Bank and the 1967 conflict during which Israeli seizure of the West Bank resulted in the exodus of an estimated 300,000 Palestinians, have all been important factors in Jordan's responses to naturalization and citizenship.[53] Following the first influx of Palestinians into Jordan and the annexation of 1950, Jordan extended full citizenship to Palestinians. In 1954 naturalization laws were passed in which a four-year residency requirement was established together with a declaration affirming that full citizenship rights would be extended to all naturalized persons. Palestinians represented around 60 per cent of Jordan's population and for strategic reasons it seemed appropriate to adopt a more liberal naturalization procedure. However, the difficulties which Jordan faced centred on the issue of citizen loyalty; that is, where precisely did the affinities of former Palestinian, newly Jordanian citizens lie. With most of the members of the Palestine National Council, the executive body of the Palestine Liberation Organization, holding Jordanian citizenship, the spectre of 'double allegiances' and the suspicion that a significant proportion of the population were indifferent or, indeed, antipathetic to the 'host' country was inevitable.[54]

The charge was made that Palestinians, irrespective of their citizenship in other countries, would always cling to their own political interests; in other words, their focus of attention would centre on the acquisition of their own homeland. As such, they would suffer a conflict of loyalties in their citizenship and this would be reflected in their political behaviour. The impact of the contradiction of being a citizen of one country whilst cleaving to the idea of another would be deleterious and result in instability, conflict, and political regression in the 'host' state. The nature of the Palestinian quest for nation-statehood has sometimes been used as a reason for denying Palestinian migrants citizenship with or without political rights. There also exists the fear that the granting of such rights would destabilize the precarious balance which often exists between the indigenous citizenry within a country, for example, the Lebanon. In a sense, the Palestinian situation appears to be similar to that of other groups of people within the Middle East and in this context the Kurdish community comes to mind. However, doubt surrounds the extent to which the Kurds' demands for self-determination within an autonomous region of say, Iraq, actually implies the break-up of Iraq. In short, citizenship can contain a community's desire for regionalism, federalism or autonomous status within a nation-state but it cannot sustain a group's affiliation to another state, be the state actual or notional. In J. S. Mill's opinion, the permanence of representative institutions depended upon 'the readiness of the people to fight for them in case of their being endangered'.[55] If the citizenry of a country are not committed to the nation they may very well undermine democratic development and retard any reforming process.

Consociationalism

In countries with deep social cleavages and political or religious differences, pluralist democracy might be under threat unless it followed a particular model, that is, the process of consociational democracy.[56] Consociationalism attempts to unite disparate groupings within society by permitting politicians representing sectional interests to govern at national level in a coalition with the leaders of other parties and groups. Thus, by modifying the oppositionist tendencies inherent in the British model of liberal democracy, 'fragmented but stable democracies' can be achieved.[57] The development of the consociational system moved the debate about democracy one stage further. It was not liberal democracy, as such, which was unsuitable for plural societies but rather the form known as the 'Westminster Model'. As soon as majority rule no longer implied the relegation of the minority to opposition benches in order to wait its turn at the next election, democracy had a chance of success. Through a system of proportional representation it would be possible for all leaders of various groups to be represented at the decision-making level. This procedure would permit all sectors of society to have a stake in the political environment of the country. The political system of the Lebanon between 1943 and 1975 was judged to fit the consociational format in that deputies were elected to the National Assembly on the basis of religious quotients.

Societal fragmentation, then, could to a certain degree be contained especially when associated with another strong characteristic of consociationalism, the separate autonomy awarded to each sect. Each sect would create its own welfare, educational and recreational organizations with a correspondingly minimal role accorded to the state within the framework of a *laissez-faire* economy. Although Lijphart maintains that consociational democracy existed in Lebanon for more than thirty years and performed satisfactorily until the political system was savaged by the effects of the civil war and its aftermath, he does acknowledge its constraints and weaknesses. One of its chief failings was the system's inflexibility and in the context of Lebanon's electoral apportionment this was a major difficulty. The confessional system as operated in Lebanon was set on a 6:5 ratio of Christian to Muslim; as such, it was always biased in favour of the Christian sects much to the chagrin of the Muslim community. Between 1943 and 1975 the Christian sector always rejected any demands for a more equitable distribution of seats. Other criticisms have been levelled at the way in which the 'elite cartel' structure became exceptionally adept at representing the 'particularistic interests of individuals, families and clans' as well as facilitating an efficient vehicle for 'patron-clientelism' based on the exchange of favours for votes.[58]

Consociationalism does, at first sight, appear to override the so-called 'mobilization of bias' in the community, that is, the dominant set of values, rituals and institutions which tend to favour the vested interest of one or more groups, relative to another. Yet Lijphart admits that the elitism of this form of democracy should not be compared with any ideal of equal power or citizen participation.[59] Its chief problem is not its 'undemocratic nature' but its 'potential failure to bring about and maintain political stability'.[60] Decision-making would be slow if not completely immobilized especially with the operation of the mutual veto. The larger the coalition the more difficult it would be to avoid stagnation and inefficiency. Lijphart concedes that the government-versus-opposition cycle has the advantage in that 'dissatisfied citizens can cast their vote against the government without voting against the regime', whilst in the consociational model the government and regime coincide, thereby turning dissatisfaction with government performance into a far more damaging 'disaffection with the regime'. The solution advocated by Lijphart is for voters to form new political parties which 'may be anti-system or anti-regime parties but not necessarily anti-democratic'.[61] Whilst the adversarial system is seen to be efficient in the short term it is likely to break down in the long run, thereby causing animosity and suspicion amongst those sections of society excluded from office; whereas the consociational model, even with all its deficiencies may create a climate more conducive to the persistence of a system of democracy, after its demise.

It is, therefore, both the form of democracy a country adopts together with its exposure to the structure's demands which serve to create a future democratic trend. Oppositionist democracy, on the other hand, may actually repel developing countries from treading the democratic path. This view contradicts Lipset's argument that once established, a democratic political system 'gathers momentum' and creates its own institutions to ensure its continued existence. Lipset maintains that even a 'premature' democracy of any form will attempt to survive by facilitating the growth of other conditions necessary for its continuation, such as autonomous private organizations.[62] Again, the debate shifts back to the form of economic base necessary to sustain a system of democracy and the extent to which a country's internal measures of economic reform may coincide with demands for greater participation and a more pluralistic style of politics.

Islam

As a result of the Iranian Islamic revolution in 1979 and the consequent resurgence of Islam as a political movement much attention has been focused on the nature of a theocratic state.[63] Although Islamic 'fundamentalism' was a term coined in the West, it was quite clear that the Sh'ia Islamic directives of Iran were both radical and formidable. Indeed, according to James Piscatori, a new dynamism embraced Islam since the late 1960s, a time when Muslims began to reaffirm the importance of their faith 'to their social and political lives.'[64] Inevitably, the renewed importance of religion in the polities of numerous states in the Middle East and elsewhere has led to an examination of the relationship between Islam and democracy. Whilst some writers point to a basic incompatibility between what might be regarded as secular democracy and the rule of God, others suggest that in traditional Islamic discourse 'tolerance, justice, fair play and universal brotherhood' were prominent features.[65] If Islam is regarded as opposed to the main elements of Western democratic tradition and is based on 'violence and intolerance' it is a view founded on misunderstanding and misinterpretation. It is possible to be both a Muslim and a democrat.[66] In this interpretation the institution of the 'Shura' is a central component of the Islamic political system. A 'Shura' is a consultative council, elected by the people. As Choudhury elaborates:

> The 'Shura' will assist and guide the Amir [leader]. It is obligatory for the Amir to administer the country with the advice of his Shura. The Amir can retain office only so long as he enjoys the confidence of the people, and must resign when he loses this confidence. Every citizen has the right to criticise the Amir and his government, and all reasonable means for the expression of public opinion should be available.[67]

If Islamic states appear not to construct their political structures in precisely this manner, Choudhury maintains that this is not the fault of Islam and its ideals in much the same way that the 'limitations and shortcomings' which may be found in some democratic states 'should not be attributed to democracy and its ideals'.[68] The notion of consultation, then, is an important component within Islam, but Ami Ayalon cautions against distinguishing a 'Shura' within a 'Majlis' (Council) as a parliament. He argues that it would be misleading to 'mistake fully sovereign Western parliaments for councils with limited advisory power'. Whilst the term 'Majlis' is used in the Middle East to denote a national assembly, Ayalon asserts it is a word 'with no traditional political connotations' and must be qualified, as in 'al-majlis al-ali' a cabinet or senate; 'majlis al-umma', a national assembly; 'majlis shura al-madaris', council of education, and so on.[69] Yet it is as well to remember that many a Western parliament has been dismissed as simply a 'talking shop' with little authority but to deliberate and advise recalcitrant leaders. The central issue here is accountability and the extent to which deputies in the Majlis al-umma represent the interests of a particular constituency or the extent to which their role is instructed by Islam. If Akbar Ahmed is correct, the central difference between the West and Islam is rooted in their two 'opposed philosophies: one based in secular materialism, the other in faith'.[70] The debate is a complex one and if the question of democratization in the Middle East were not considered to be so important it might not have begun. In other words, if 'democracy' was considered to be so trivial a concept, associated with Western imperialism and holding little meaning in Islamic society, there would exist no imperative to attempt to connect the two 'opposing philosophies'. It is precisely because democracy is attractive to the peoples of the Middle East, peoples who wish to form political parties, vote in elections for a variety of different candidates, hold their representatives accountable, in short to avail themselves of political rights and responsibilities, that democracy is being discussed at this time.

The Cold War

The impact of the Cold War on the political systems of the Middle East, be they Arab, Persian (Iranian) or Israeli, has been especially penetrating.

In a global environment of superpower rivalry the Middle East assumed great significance. The West's dependence on oil supplies and policy of containment of the former Soviet Union coloured and conditioned political attitudes towards the region. Also the existence of strong communist parties in a number of states in the area coupled with the fact that the Soviet Union's own oil resources liberated its room for manoeuvre, contributed considerable tension to a relationship which was already fraught. As subsequent chapters demonstrate, scarcely a country in the area escaped the effects of the Cold War on its political structures. The curious associations of the communist parties, the support of puppet regimes by the two superpowers, the organized coups d'état and the debilitating, polarizing Arab/Israeli conflicts all combined to undermine political reform, and further entrenched an atmosphere of distrust and animosity.

The end of the Cold War, therefore, is of enormous importance to the Middle East and may be a harbinger of a new form of political potential. The lid has been taken off the political cauldron of the region. Theories of socialist democracy contained in the one-party state model and sustainable in a classless society were previously justified and partly explained by the existence of the Soviet model of development. The efficacy of the one-party state in both economic and political terms has been questioned. Democracy is now defined as pluralistic with elections characterized by competition, participation and representation. The ideals of human rights and freedom of the individual are in the ascendancy rather than discussion of collective goals and nation-state building. The states of the Middle East may now enjoy new possibilities of political autonomy, responsibility and accountability.

To draw this chapter to a close it is necessary to explain the organization of the chapters and the reasons why certain countries have been chosen for investigation. The arrangement of the country studies reflects the region's political diversity. The differentiated categorization of *monarchical/dynastic state*; *theocratic state*; *dominant party state*; *multi-party state* and *consociational state*, permits an examination of varied political structures and the process by which political change can occur in specific countries. It will be evident that the study does not solely concentrate on Arab states in what Michael Hudson describes as the pan-Arab core, but includes chapters on Iran and Israel.

The case studies were chosen to reveal the interlocking nature of some factors in the region. The following chapter examines Jordan and Kuwait which have in common profound problems of demography and citizenship which are presenting a challenge to both rulers.

Population mobility is such an important issue in the area that its impact on developing and developed political systems alike has to be assessed in order to determine the extent to which it is destabilizing and retarding. Chapter 3 considers the case of the Islamic Republic of Iran, a non-Arab state, but one which has suffered the consequences of the Cold War. This chapter looks at the nature of a theocratic state in order to assess whether or not it differs substantially from other modes of government. It also focuses attention on the debate surrounding the question of Islamic democracy. Chapter 4 examines two states within a certain category, the dominant party states of Iraq and Syria which have evolved rather differently. Far from being united by their dual Ba'ath Parties they are, in fact, estranged by their existence. In considering the separate case studies of Israel and Lebanon there are, of course, very different patterns of democratic political expression. Some of the countries under investigation have been and, indeed, still are profoundly threatened by their neighbours, and at times particular actions have wrought deep fissures within those countries' political structures. Equally, external pressure has been brought to bear on a number of states which has further debilitated or undermined reform. In short, and at the risk of sounding as if a conundrum is being presented, the states under study are different in the ordering of their political systems but they share a spectre of common features which have deeply affected their political advancement.

The monarchical/dynastic state – Jordan and Kuwait

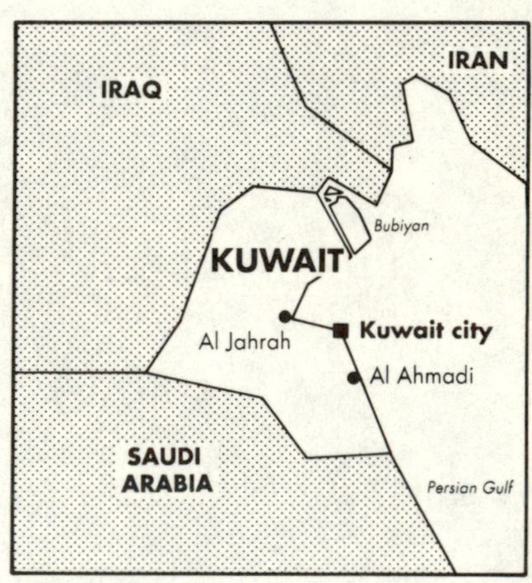

In any comparative approach to political analysis Kuwait and Jordan offer a stimulating study. Vastly different in economic terms, one excessively rich, the other largely impoverished, the two countries do, however, share distinct commonalities which underpin the rationale for examining them jointly. Both share long-lasting dynastic systems; both contend with acute problems of population mobility and minority status for their indigenous population and both are particularly vulnerable to powerful neighbours. These factors have played an especially important role in the countries' respective development of political processes and practices and any understanding of democratization must take account of these powerful forces; forces which, of course, are not necessarily confined to the Third World.

This chapter considers Jordan and Kuwait separately but intends to draw parallels between the two political systems. Both case studies look at the institution and experience of a parliament or national assembly. The associated question of citizenship, first raised in Chapter 1 will now be fully explored. The overwhelming impact of the Arab-Israeli conflict in terms of the massive transfer of Palestinian peoples will be examined as will the political ramifications of such a movement on the polity of Jordan. The 'rentier state' analysis will be further considered in the context of Kuwait, a country which has been regarded as fitting the model rather well, in order to discover whether or not it explains the current political climate. The various political advances, moves towards greater liberalization and possible democratization and the obstacles which often stymied such developments will be analysed. Finally, the post-1991 Gulf War period which has heralded a discussion of political reform, will be assessed.

The Hashemite Kingdom of Jordan

Since the end of the 1991 Gulf War Jordan's commitment to the establishment of a pluralistic democracy seems unambiguous. Various statements have been made by King Hussein and Crown Prince Hasan outlining the priorities facing the country. According to Crown Prince Hasan, in October 1991 only 'Democratisation, freedom of expression, human rights and the accountability of rulers will provide a route towards the political economy of peace, security and progress.'[1] Politics was to be an arena in which 'people matter and where peoples' aspirations and humanitarian considerations are paramount'. Some four months previously the King pronounced that the nation's political objectives were clearly defined: the government would embark on 'implementing political pluralism, including a law on publications and licensing political parties'. Democracy was not to be regarded as merely a country's institutions, it represented a 'general approach and way of life'. As such, courses on democracy, including its rules, norms and responsibilities, would be taught in various educational and cultural institutions. In the final analysis, 'democratisation would require all people to abide and respect the law'.[2]

These statements unquestionably have an uplifting quality, producing an immediate impression of political reform and liberalization but it must be remembered there are two fundamental issues which have beset Jordan's political advancement for over forty years: namely the two-pronged elements of the Palestinian question, territory and immigration. When in 1946, Transjordan emerged as a fully independent nation-state, it was only five years before the country had changed its name; enlarged its territory; and increased its population. The influences which were prevalent during those early years still continue to be a focus of preoccupation and attention. Jordan's tense relationship with its neighbour, Israel, the evolving aspirations of the Palestinians, and its complicated demographic structure have all remained constant factors and, more importantly, have made their impact on the country's political direction Since 1952 Jordan has not experienced extended periods of democratic rule and it is necessary to consider whether the contemporary political climate is likely to be more conducive to the formation of a pluralistic mode of government.

Constitution/parliament

Transjordan's first experience of constitutional government occurred in 1928, courtesy of the British, who granted the area autonomy in 1923. Previously, the territory had been included in the League of Nation's Mandate for Palestine, which was administered by Britain. The 1928 constitution although seemingly democratic in form proved to be less so in content. In fact, it enabled King Abdullah (the Amir), whose pre-eminence had been established by the colonial powers, Britain and France in the wake of the First World War, to retain his dominant position over the government. He was empowered to appoint and dismiss all six members of the Executive Council; could exert authority over the 22 member Legislative Council from which the Executive Council was formed and could dismiss Parliament at will and rule by martial law. Oppositionists to the Amir and the British, convened a congress in the capital, Amman, and adopted a national pact proclaiming their country a sovereign, independent, constitutional Arab state.

The nationalists boycotted the first elections held in September 1928 and the King duly declared martial law. It was an inauspicious beginning for even a truncated form of democracy and there was little change until full Independence was gained in May 1946. It is difficult to estimate the importance of the 1928 constitution in terms of developing a political tradition within the country because as Michael Hudson points out the British still exercised 'the last word on foreign affairs and [a] decisive influence over the treasury'.[3] The second Constitution of 1946, divided the Legislative Council into a House of Deputies and a House of Notables which gave the appearance of a functioning bicameral system but still left a significant degree of control with the King. He could appoint both the upper house and his cabinet. The lower house had no legislative facility, that being the reserve of the cabinet. There existed a belief amongst Arab nationalists that the King remained too closely linked with the British in that the country depended on Britain for financial assistance and had a British general in command of its armed forces.[4] However, if British interference was an irritant both during the period of colonial rule and shortly after Independence, a new and more agonized relationship would envelop the political life of newly independent Transjordan, affecting both its Constitutional framework and its national assembly. That troubled association was to be with its neighbour, Palestine.

In the first flush of Britain's post-war divestment of colonial responsibility the Palestine Mandate was to prove to be the most difficult. By 1947 the rash and conflicting promises Britain had made thirty years earlier to the Arabs and Jews as to their mutual claims to the land finally rebounded on the British to the point that Palestine had become practically ungovernable.[5]

Britain referred the issue to the United Nations and on 29 November 1947, that newly formed organization voted in favour of the partition of Palestine into two states, one Arab, the other Jewish. The option of partition had been raised in 1937 but the British then retreated from implementing the policy by military force. Ten years later, retreat became withdrawal and Britain announced that it would take no part in implementing the United Nations resolution. Britain left Palestine on 14 May 1948 and the first Arab-Israeli war began on 15 May 1948.

Transjordan had hoped to gain from this conflict in that it expected to enlarge its territory to include the section of Palestine which had been designated as the proposed Palestinian state.[6] Events did not turn out this way. Jewish forces were stronger than anticipated and the claims of the majority of states in the Arab League were for the whole of unpartitioned Palestine. Nevertheless, Jordan gained central Palestine, that is the West Bank of the River Jordan and East Jerusalem which it subsequently annexed in 1950. Although the annexation expanded Jordan's boundaries it created demographic changes which were profound. Partition, both the threat of it and the actual war had displaced the Palestinian Arabs. Unwanted in Israel and having denied themselves a truncated state of their own in their absolute rejection of the UN plan, they fled to neighbouring lands. After the 1948/49 war, the Palestinians were in an even more difficult position; not only had they lost the territory which had been apportioned to the Jews, but also the boundaries of the Jewish state had expanded to include land deemed to be part of the Palestinian Arab state. The estimated figure of displaced Palestinians was 700,000[7] and whilst a significant number had relocated to the Jordanian-occupied West Bank, many had actually moved into Jordan, especially Amman, whose population increased from 60,000 in 1945 to approximately 200,000 by the early 1950s.[8] In short, then, Jordan's population increased by almost two-thirds, thus radically altering the polity and more significantly, making the Jordanians a minority in their extended state. It was inevitable that such demographic changes would present a challenge to Jordan's fragile political structures. The question was, how could the country's vastly expanded population be embraced within its political life. The obvious solution was to invite the Palestinians to vote in Jordan's national elections and this, in fact, occurred in 1950.

Palestinian representation

The elections of 1950 were notable in that they resulted in a new 11-member cabinet which included five Palestinians. Yet relations between the Palestinians and the Jordanians were uneasy. King Abdullah's offer of Jordanian citizenship to all Palestinians, living in either the East or the West Bank, was rejected as an opportunistic ploy designed to subjugate the Palestinians under the King's rule. Ultimately, in Jerusalem in July 1951, the King was assassinated by supporters of the Palestinian leader, the Mufti. Abdullah's successor, his son, King Talal, presided over the promulgation of a new constitution which was more liberal in disposition, in that it afforded parliament greater powers. It was, perhaps, inevitable that a new constitution should attempt to deflect any further potential conflict and this is precisely what the new constitution aimed to achieve. Its provisions, for that time and even if viewed by contemporary standards, were wide-ranging and possibly unrealistic: guarantees to the right of employment; protection of labour by fair wages, hours and unemployment compensation and rules concerning health and welfare, but they suggest an understanding of the depth of the difficulties confronting Jordan. The constitution divided cabinet and parliamentary seats equally between the Jordanians and the Palestinians but as the Palestinians were in the majority it was apparent that whilst they might gain social and economic benefits they would be asked to sacrifice political rights. In a sense, the Palestinians adopted a Janus-faced position; on the one hand claiming the whole of un-partitioned Palestine but on the other, seeking greater representation and control in Jordan, a country they were obliged to inhabit.

The political rights of the Palestinians in Jordan raises interesting questions: first, the issue of nation-statehood and second, the nature of pan-Arabism. The Palestinians' territorial affinity with Palestine was, of course, long standing, but the issue which demands attention is the extent to which Jordan had a clear focus of what it perceived to be the demands of a nation-state. It is a commonly held view that countries emerging from colonial rule, with their terrritorial dimensions hapharzardly drawn, have lacked a strong sense of nationality and statehood. Nation-state building was often a clarion cry of many newly independent states in the 1950s and 1960s. However, in the case of Jordan it is clear that a distinct demarcation line had been drawn between the Palestinians and the indigenous Jordanian peoples, as exampled by the granting of fewer political rights for the immigrant Palestinian community than for the Jordanian population. Had a real sense of nation-statehood not existed it might be imagined that peoples – immigrants – could come and go as they pleased. Citizenship then, was recognized as an essential feature of the Jordanian state. This attitude also casts doubt on the assumption that primordial loyalties could act as a synthetic glue in uniting Arab peoples and forging a singular Arab Nation. There existed real differences between the Palestinians and Jordanians, not only in their dialects or dispositions but in the fact that they both possessed a strong notion of statehood. Otherwise the fact that the Palestinians formed a majority of the population in Jordan would have been regarded as a development of no importance and the Palestinians would have been dutifully accorded the appropriate dispensations. As it was the issue of majority-minorityhood between Palestinians and Jordanians and their respective political loyalties became increasingly important factors which ultimately contributed to a damaging civil war. It is difficult to imagine a constitution or a national assembly accommodating such a large demographic change in a country's polity without actually changing the nature of the state itself. Jordan had, of course, almost become a Palestinian state; Palestinian Arabs formed the majority of the population and were constitutionally entitled to equal representation in parliament. Yet Jordan was not the Palestinian homeland; the Palestinian peoples had been detached from their own territory which they hoped to regain from the vantage point of Jordanian land. In short, if Jordan appeared a little uneasy about the direction of Palestinian political affinities, the Palestinians had no desire to become long-term Jordanian citizens; their chief objective was to regain their land and any commitment to another state's nationality would dilute their own claims.

Arab/Israeli conflict

On the eve of the 1967 war with Israel the political tide in Jordan was less than calm. Syria and Egypt were attempting to incite the population to revolt against King Hussein, who had assumed the throne in 1953; a series of rapid cabinet changes had followed the assassination of Prime Minister, Hazza al-Majali a few years earlier, and Jordan had suspended support for the secretary of the Palestine Liberation Organization (PLO) following accusations of pro-communist leanings. If Jordan entered the war in an unstable condition it emerged from the conflict practically on the verge of collapse. By the end of the Six Day War, all territory west of the River Jordan had been occupied by Israeli troops and Jordan again witnessed the influx of refugees estimated to be in the region of between 150,000 and 250,000 persons.[9] Jordan had lost a tract of land that was vital and had substantially increased its refugee population. These two factors created economic and social difficulties but the political challenge came from the activities of Palestinian groups who were gaining control over the refugee camps. The King feared the creation of a state within a state which would challenge his authority internally in the form of riots and demonstrations and externally in the shape of attacks from Israel.

The destabilization of Jordan was favoured in some quarters within Israel. In the World Zionist Organization's publication, *Kivunim*, a former senior foreign ministry official, Oded Yinon, proclaimed that 'Israel's policy in peace and war ought to be directed at the liquidation of Jordan under the present regime and the transfer of power to the Palestinian majority . . . accelerating the emigration of Palestinians from the West to the East Bank.'[10] In government circles it was no secret that in certain sectors existed the belief that 'the Palestinians should be encouraged to overthrow the Hashemite Kingdom and convert Jordan into their own national state'.[11] Certainly, Palestinian groups were gaining confidence and it was only a matter of time before the violence in Jordan flared into a civil war which began in September 1970. By 1971, the King announced that the Palestinian guerrilla problem had been 'solved', their bases had been destroyed and 2500 had been captured. The PLO's presence in Jordan was reduced to 'a representative's office, a social security and pensions office, and a battalion of the Palestinian Liberation Army firmly under Jordanian army control'.[12]

Reprisal attacks, however, continued to be made against members of the Jordanian government outside the country. On 28 September 1971 the Prime Minister was assassinated in Cairo by members of a Palestinian group, the Black September Organization. One of the central criticisms made by Palestinian organizations of the Jordanian monarchy and the country's political structure was its pro-Western, undemocratic, ultra-conservative form which held the nation in thrall to the King. Some comments were justified; political parties had been proscribed for over ten years; martial law had been in operation since 1967 and in September 1971 King Hussein had formed the Jordanian National Union (renamed the Arab National Union in 1972) which was designed to take the place of political parties. Advocates of so-called 'imported ideologies', that is, those supporting the beliefs of the communists, Ba'athists, Nasserists and Palestinian nationalists, were denied membership. The union was to be Jordan's only legal political organization and accordingly the King appointed himself President and his brother, the Crown Prince, vice-President, and chose members of the Supreme Executive Council. These developments portray a dispiriting picture of political life in Jordan at that time but they must be viewed within a context of constraints, one of which was the Cold War.

Elections held in 1956 resulted in the success of the National Socialists, a pro-Nasser and anti-Western party, led by Sulaiman Nabulsi, which won 13 of the 20 parliamentary seats. As a result of this victory financial aid was sought from the Arab states, principally Saudi Arabia, Egypt and Syria and overtures were made to the Soviet Union in an attempt to establish diplomatic relations. It was this move which excited the interest of the United States, freshly vigilant with the Congress-approved 'Eisenhower Doctrine', which had been designed to provide military and economic assistance to Middle Eastern countries threatened by 'international communism'. Nabulsi was charged with anti-monarchical sentiments and dismissed; political parties were suppressed and American loans of US$50 million per annum began to arrive.[13] Jordan was aligned with Western interests which inevitably created division with those countries more closely associated with the Soviet Union, that is, Syria, Iraq and Egypt. Political parties, therefore, were judged to be dangerous and potentially destabilizing, both from a Cold War perspective and also from a regional dimension.

King Hussein's position, then, in the early 1970s was still uneasy despite attempts at stabilization. In March 1972 he proposed the establishment of a United Arab Kingdom as a solution to the Arab-Israeli conflict. The Kingdom would be integrated into a federal state with a Jordanian region, Amman, serving as both its capital and federal capital, and a Palestinian region, with Jerusalem as its capital. Each region was to be virtually autonomous, with a federal council of ministers under the jurisdiction of the King. This scheme succeeded in arousing opposition from all the interested parties: the Palestinian organizations, Israel and Egypt, and it was not long before Jordan's neighbours broke off relations and the country became regionally isolated. This was coupled with an attempted military coup in

Amman in November 1972. A few months later Abu Daoud, one of the leaders of the Palestinian group al-Fatah and 16 other members, were arrested on charges of infiltrating into Jordan for the purpose of subversive activities. It was not until October 1974 that the political situation in Jordan became less tense, the reason for which emanated from the meeting of the Arab Summit Conference at Rabat at which representatives of 20 Arab heads of state recognized the 'right of the Palestinian people to establish an independent national authority, under the leadership of the PLO, in its capacity as the sole legitimate representative of the Palestinian people, over all liberated territory'.[14] By agreeing to the resolution, Hussein took a radical and politically significant step. Jordan had effectively ceded its claim to represent the Palestinians and to re-incorporate the West Bank into the Hashemite Kingdom and by so doing was no longer obliged to maintain Palestinian representation. This being so immediately following the Rabat Conference, the King dissolved parliament with the intention of reorganizing and thus reducing the level of Palestinian presence in the executive and legislative branches of government. Elections were postponed in March 1975 and when parliament was briefly reconvened in February 1976 a constitutional amendment was enacted to suspend elections indefinitely.

Economic factors

The demographic configuration within Jordan was crucial for whilst many Palestinians had become Jordanian citizens there now existed a real doubt about where their allegiances rested: with the PLO or with Jordan under King Hussein. Yet Jordan was to find the Palestinian population beneficial to the economy. Between 1976 and 1980 Jordan's gross domestic product grew by 62 per cent in real terms.[15] The increase was not due to a surge in the productive capacity of the country's natural resources but was based on the economic largesse of the Arab oil-producing states flushed with their new found wealth resulting from the oil price rises of 1973/74.

Jordan's economy had always depended on external assistance, particularly after the loss of the West Bank, but its relationship with the oil-producing states now carried important political overtones. Jordan's primary source of foreign exchange was the income received from members of its population working outside the country, largely in the Gulf states. During the late 1970s the remittance income generated by this form of activity stood at US$1.1 billion, far in excess of the country's visible exports of US$450 million. Apart from the obvious benefits to the economy of labour migration there was another important element: the majority of those working abroad were Palestinian. Suddenly Jordan's boast that its manpower was the country's greatest natural resource assumed a new meaning. Not only were the Palestinians now an economic asset contributing significantly towards the well-being of the country, but also, many were no longer actually living in Jordan. There could scarcely be a more attractive economic and political equation.

It might seem paradoxical that despite the economic rights contained in Jordan's constitution, i.e., the right to work, the right of ownership, etc. there were no major land reforms or redistributive taxation policies introduced after the loss of the West Bank. One major reason for this absence was the numerical imbalance between Palestinians and Jordanians and the doubts this raised about which community would benefit. Certainly, since 1967 Jordanian strategy had been coloured by one essential ingredient: fear; the fear that Israel would eventually de-populate the West Bank of its Arab population and expel them across the border into Jordan, thereby opening up internal dissension and threatening the King's position. Consequently, it was Hussein's policy to keep an extremely tight rein over the political life of the country. In April 1978 he formed, by royal Decree, a 60-member National Consultative Council which effectively suspended all participatory political activity. This was as close to a 'Shura' as he considered possible at the time, but this is not to suggest that the Jordanian populace was completely de-politicized.

Political awareness

A study of the predominantly Jordanian town of Al-Karak, conducted in 1968, found that the local people either 'individually or as members of the town's government office, advisory councils and committees, exercised significant influence on central government'. The study discovered that certain procedures were followed when central government agreement was required for a local policy: the plans would be formulated and presented to central government for approval and then lobbying would take place through bureaucratic channels and contacts. Although there was no question as to the level and extent of independent power and superiority retained by central government, it was important, the study proposed, that it should be seen as a body within the political structure which 'not only acts upon others but is also acted upon by them.'[16] With regard to the parliamentary elections held in 1967 it was found that despite the absence of political parties, individual candidates running for office entered into agreements with each other in order to campaign as a group and to exchange various kinds of support. In Al-Karak all four successful candidates were united on one ticket and despite dubious procedural arrangements surrounding the election, the impression gained is not one of a completely subjugated population unable to engage in any political activity.[17] In fact, it reveals a nascent form of political involvement at the local level with a quite advanced interplay between local communities and central government.

The town of Al-Karak stands in sharp relief to the activities of the Palestinian organizations and their heightened level of politicization but, nevertheless, it was the peoples of Al-Karak who over twenty years later, were to demand political reforms from the government. In 1989 community leaders in Karak submitted an appeal outlining points which were to become the basis of nationally endorsed demands, including: the amendment of the electoral law to provide democratic pluralist parliament representation; the granting of more political freedoms and a freer press and the formulation of a national economic programme. One of the significant factors in these demands is that they emanated from the Jordanian population irrespective of their Palestinian or Jordanian heritage. The Karak programme of demands gained real momentum when they were adopted by the Amman-based elected leaders of the country's professional associations, who promptly contacted Crown Prince Hassan. In what can only be described as being part of the domestic push to democratization in the late 1980s, the monarchy was warned that the way in which the country was being ruled was unacceptable to Jordanian people: 'This small country, whose very entity is threatened, is looking forward to a change in the leadership's attitude . . . Governments have shrunk in role and influence, yet at the same time have grown in tyranny.'[18] In a sense, political life in Jordan had begun to liberalize in the early 1980s but this shift had more to do with external pressures associated with the Arab-Israeli peace talks, than the freeing up of indigenous demands.

External pressures

Soon after the election of US President, Ronald Reagan a new Arab-Israeli peace initiative was announced, and King Hussein was privately consulted about the proposal. In the Reagan Plan, Jordan was pivotal for it proposed that 'self-government by the Palestinians of the West Bank and Gaza in association with Jordan offers the best chance for a durable, just and lasting peace.'[19] Negotiations took place in Washington and Amman and the King declared his willingness to cooperate but only in so far as a settlement would be acceptable to majority opinion among all interested parties. Yasser Arafat, leader of the Palestine Liberation Organization rejected the proposal and the plan was dropped. However, there were encouraging signs in that Arafat and Hussein's talks had been cordial and the Americans seemed amenable in terms of supplying economic aid. It is difficult to know whether the King's decision to recall the National Assembly and to hold the first elections in the country for 17 years was a result of private pressure brought to bear by an American government, sensitive in the post-Iranian revolution period to charges of propping-up undemocratic regimes in the Middle East, or to a domestic decision taken in a seemingly more conciliatory political climate. Most probably both factors were important. In any case, the election held on 12 March 1984, although welcome as, of course, any elections are after such a long moratorium, was not a full parliamentary one and was conducted without political parties which remained firmly banned. However, one new feature was introduced: women were enfranchised for the first time.

The results of the election revealed support for the Muslim Brotherhood, an Islamic organization which had been permitted to participate as a non-political 'da'wa' (evangelical) movement. In the absence of formal political parties it is perhaps inevitable that Islamic movements assumed a political complexion, not only in Jordan but also in other states in the Middle East. Had the electorate been allowed to cast their votes for a variety of political parties, the Muslim Brotherhood might not have been so popular. As it was ministers began giving public sermons in mosques outlining their preference for the establishment of Islamic rule in the country. As the rights of the individual contained in the Constitution allowed for the toleration of all religions, preaching and calling for the institution of Islamic rule was judged to be almost an act of sedition. For the King, this sortie into such a minimal aspect of democratic activity had proved to be unsettling, nevertheless relations between Arafat and Hussein appeared to be improving.

Talks between the two men led to an agreement on a framework for a possible peace initiative in February 1985 and for a time it seemed a positive move. Both leaders advocated that peace talks should take the form of an international conference, comprising the five permanent members of the United Nations Security Council and all parties to the conflict, including the PLO. The initiative favoured an approach in which Palestinian people would exercise their right to self-determination within a confederate state between Jordan and Palestine. However, a series of events were to take place which thwarted this so-called 'historic achievement': three Israelis were killed in Larnaca, Cyprus in September 1985; the PLO headquarters in Tunis was bombed in October and later that month, the Italian cruise-ship the *Archille Lauro* was hijacked by members of the PLO and a Jewish-American passenger died. The consequent breakdown of these negotiations once again raised the question of Jordan's stability *vis-à-vis* the Palestinians and Israel and renewed the old dilemmas. The King could either accept the military imperatives of the PLO and allow it the necessary freedom of action thereby rendering Jordan vulnerable to Israeli reprisal attacks or he could confront the PLO and its supporters and in so doing create a hot-bed of unrest within Jordan itself.[17] An additional anxiety lay in the belief that the United States would eventually agree with elements within the Israeli government and decide that the Hashemites were dispensable. Although there is no indication that this was the position in 1985/86 it is clear that American policy-makers had always included in their analysis of the Arab/Israeli dispute the possibility of Jordan being destabilized, especially if, as one scenario predicted, Israel formally annexed the West Bank and Jordan became the Palestinian state.[20]

The Palestinian Uprising (Intifada) against Israeli occupation began in December 1987 and it was to have a profound impact on Jordan. Although public demonstrations in Jordan in support of the Intifada were controlled by security precautions, it was not long before Amman received a series of bomb attacks. The Palestinian group, Black September, claimed responsibility and accused Jordan of being a 'client Zionist regime'.[21] Jordan again saw itself as being threatened. The Intifada quickly turned into an eloquent expression of the strong Palestinian identity of the people of the West

Bank and Gaza and rapidly attracted international attention. Furthermore, and more worryingly for Hussein, the uprising and its leadership projected hostility towards Jordan. The Arab League summit held in 1988 confirmed this tendency and hailed the 'heroic' Intifada, endorsed the establishment of an independent Palestinian state in the West Bank and Gaza and insisted on the participation of the PLO in peace talks. Clearly, the Intifada created a new set of conditions in which Jordan could no longer realistically attract Palestinian support away from the PLO and promote itself as an alternative. If the Palestinians were to support the PLO as their sole representative, Hussein and his government decided, they would have to come to terms with the practical implications of their demands for an independent Palestinian state; in short, Jordan would disengage from the West Bank.

In July 1988 Jordan cancelled its $1300 million Development Plan for the West Bank which had been opposed by the PLO, and severed its legal and administrative links with the territory. This action held implications for Jordan's domestic political structure. The House of Representatives was dissolved on the grounds that Palestinian representatives for the West Bank still occupied 30 of the 60 seats. This move alarmed many Jordanians who regarded parliament, mostly moribund and unrepresentative though it was, as still an important forum and a minimal expression of democratic life. Hussein, however, was engaged in political gamesmanship; by dissolving the Lower House and removing Jordanian civil servants and teachers from their administrative functions in the West Bank, Hussein had refrained from pushing separation to its limits. He had not formally and irrevocably repealed the 'union agreement' of 1950 which united the East and West Banks and according to the 1952 Constitution, the West Bank remained part of the Hashemite Kingdom. By not pursuing this line of action he was managing to leave himself the option of reconsideration. In reality, of course, the Jordanian legislature, such as it was, had exercised little or no practical influence over the affairs of the West Bank since 1967 and Israel soon introduced measures to restrict the activities of Palestinian institutions so as to prevent the PLO from filling the administrative vacuum created by the Jordanian exodus.

It was believed that by placing responsibility for the West Bank firmly in the hands of the PLO the Palestinian population would discover its inability to finance and administer public services. The Jordanian government decreed that Palestinians residing in the West Bank were no longer to be considered Jordanian citizens. Although they would still be entitled to hold a Jordanian passport, in effect this would carry no formal status and would only serve as a 'travel document'. This was seen to be an important decision as most of the members of the Palestine National Council, the executive body of the PLO, were Jordanian citizens. It also provided a sharper edge to the Jordanian charge of Palestinian 'double allegiances'.

Nevertheless, Hussein was walking a political tightrope. There was no certainty that the Palestinians would not blame the Jordanian government for punishing them for supporting the PLO. One American department official claimed that the King's objective was to prove the PLO to be practically incompetent and hope that 'the people of the West Bank will see the light and come running back to him. Eventually, it is hoped, the West Bank Palestinians will come to their senses and may decide that the ultimate solution is a confederation of the West Bank with Jordan.'[22] But this statement begs the question of Jordan's commitment to the West Bank. Although the King's 'romantic attachment' to the West Bank is well known, certain Jordanians within the government and bureaucracy, including elements within the Royal Family are not so firmly committed: 'West Bankers do not want us, so why should we police them for the Israelis and the Americans.' The consensus of opinion among this group maintains that Jordan should concentrate on consolidating its cross cultural nation, east of the river, and establish the 'survival of a state where pluralism is a feature of excellence'.[23]

Whatever the motives underlying Hussein's decision: tactical move; fit of 'pique' with the PLO or genuine withdrawal, a momentum had been set and events were carried by it. In August 1988 legislative elections were postponed pending the revision of the now inapplicable electoral laws. King Hussein announced his intention to recognize a Palestinian government-in-exile if the Palestine National Council (PNC) should decide to establish such a body. By November 1988 the PNC proclaimed the establishment of an independent state of Palestine and, for the first time, endorsed the United Nations Security Council's Resolution 242 as a basis for a Middle East peace settlement, thus implicitly recognizing the state of Israel. Jordan immediately recognized the new state and a month later Arafat addressing the United Nations General Assembly, renounced violence on behalf of the PLO.

Indigenous pressures

Although Jordan seemed to have detached itself from the West Bank successfully, domestically tensions were rising which would lead to what commentators at the time referred to as Jordan's own 'intifada'. Already in 1985/86 Jordan's external tensions had been reflected in domestic unrest in the form of student protests and demonstrations at Yarmouk University. The unrest at that time was significant for two reasons. First, the university included a higher percentage of Palestinian students from the Israeli-occupied territories and second, the manner in which the government overreacted pointed to a clear lack of communication between students, the university administration and the government. The events at Yarmouk were seen to reflect in microcosm the political conditions in the country as a whole. Two factors combined, the tension created by the breakdown of political coordination between Jordan and the PLO and the resultant suppression of any form of protest. The Yarmouk demonstrations resulted in the deaths and injuries which aroused wide criticism especially when government actions were viewed from the wider perspective of the general repression on freedom of expression operating within the country. Whilst the government blamed so-called 'trouble-makers', the proscribed Jordanian Communist Party and the Muslim Brotherhood, the strict control of the local press, the banning of a number of journalists and the use of riot police to stem opposition, pointed to a recourse to an increasingly repressive state apparatus.

This form of unrest was a precursor for the violent demonstrations which took place in 1988/89 but these later actions were fuelled by both economic and political imperatives. The grievances were two-fold: a reaction against the dissolution of parliament and the amending of the electoral laws, and resentment at the stringency of the economic reform plan which had resulted in price rises of between 15 per cent and 50 per cent on basic goods and services. The economic programme which aroused pleas for social justice and democracy had been caused by government attempts to accommodate the rigorous demands of the International Monetary Fund (IMF) foreign debt re-scheduling plan. Paradoxically, the government had rather more options at the political level than on the economic front. More importantly, political reforms were necessary if the government was to be able to unite the country to face stringent economic measures. The government was bound to the International Monetary Fund economic reform programme and it, therefore, had to create an atmosphere of confidence in the credibility of governmental policies which would undoubtedly involve a relaxation of the curbs on freedom of expression and political rights. Also, the Karak programme, as mentioned earlier revealed that after the initial outburst of anger and violence, the polity had now transformed itself into realistic and responsible sobriety. The demands being made were both legitimate and reasonable and King Hussein had the prescience to recognize the implications for his own rule.

Jordanian society was, of course, changing in many ways. In 1985, 75 per cent of the population were literate compared with only 47 per cent in 1970. Also, there had been a dramatic improvement in health care reflected in the massive drop in the under-five mortality rate: from 218 per 1000 in 1960 to 57 per 1000 in 1988. When coupled with the fact that, on 1990 figures, 66 per cent of the people lived in urban areas and around half the population owned either a radio or a TV, all the indicators suggested that despite Jordan's relative economic poverty it had clearly developed modernizing tendencies.[24] However, one factor affecting political advancement in a number of Third World states in the late twentieth century, unlike the period immediately following their independence, is the role played by the media. According to Akbar Ahmed the media defines, 'the dominant global civilisation of our time' in that people have access to wider spheres of information. Also, the manner in which the media processes that information tends to re-orientate traditional modes of social behaviour and conduct.[25] The old benchmarks of development, particularly, adult literacy rates, are no longer so important in the process of gaining access to ideas and news, when all TV and radio demand of the population is its ability to see and listen. The impact of the media, as yet unquantified, may be a new determinant of political change and moves towards democratization.

Parliamentary elections were held in November 1989 with a record turn-out of 63 per cent of the electorate. Again the results revealed considerable gains by the Muslim Brotherhood. The broadly pro-government forces made up of 'traditionalists, rural community leaders, former officials and bedouin leaders' won only 31 of the 80 seats.[26] The remaining seats were won by independent Islamists allied to the Muslim Brotherhood, Palestinian and Arab nationalist candidates. A candidate affiliated to the Jordan Communist Party won a seat. The Muslim Brotherhood, of course, was the only 'opposition' grouping; no political parties had been permitted to participate, but as has been seen, often individuals would act in concert with each other or would operate in affiliation with an organization. In other words, oppositionists could be represented even though parties were proscribed. However, the fact that the Muslim Brotherhood was an 'official' participant may have distorted the level of support it received, especially in light of the fact that during its campaign it called for non-payment of foreign debt.

On the face of it the outcome of the election seemed a pretty daunting challenge to the King and he readily admitted there had been positive and negative aspects, yet liberalizing policies did emerge. By April 1990, Hussein had appointed a 60-member Royal Commission whose task it was to draw up a national charter to regulate political life in Jordan. The move seemed to be further evidence of the King's determination to press ahead with his 'democratic experiment'. The composition of the Commission suggested conciliatory moves were being made. The inclusion of members of the Muslim Brotherhood and left-wingers effectively stifled criticism that the charter might actually be used to limit political activity. In fact, the reverse seemed to be taking place. Throughout the Spring of 1990 a series of meetings took place between government ministers and Palestinian groups. King Hussein met leaders of the Jordanian People's Democratic Party, the Jordanian section of the Democratic Front for the Liberation of Palestine for the first time since 1970. Meetings also took place with representatives of the Jordanian Communist Party. It was suspected at the time that preparatory steps were being taken towards the removal of the ban on political parties. Certainly, for the first time in years, Jordan seemed to be securing an element of political understanding and reform when an event took place which overshadowed all progress: Iraq invaded Kuwait.

The Gulf War 1991

Iraq's invasion of Kuwait in August 1990 placed Jordan in an invidious position. Whilst the PLO and the Palestinians rallied behind the Iraqi leader, Saddam Hussein, Jordan had, only a few month's earlier, signed a trade protocol with Iraq for US$800 million and had received a promise of aid for the sum of US$50 million. Relations between Jordan and Iraq were unquestionably close. Indeed, as far back as 1985, the then Jordanian Foreign Minister, Taher al-Masri, asserted that Jordan's ties with Iraq 'cannot be shaken.'[27] According to a United Nations Relief and Works Agency report, 930,000 Palestinian refugees were resident in Jordan, under the Agency's field of operation, at the time of the Gulf crisis.[28]

In a televised address broadcast on 6 February 1991 King Hussein paid tribute to the 'heroic army of Iraq and Iraq's steadfast and courageous people', and made no mention of the plight of Kuwait. The speech was interpreted by President Bush in a statement made two days later, as a signal that Jordan had abandoned its neutral stance and had 'moved over, way over, to Saddam Hussein's camp'.[29] Consequently, the US administration confirmed its decision to place under review the aid package to Jordan worth some US$107 million. Although Jordan continued to receive aid from Japan and Germany which helped offset the impact of the US decision it was estimated at the end of February 1990 that the confrontation in the Gulf had up to that time cost the country around US$8000 million, which represented double the value of Jordan's annual domestic economic output. Before the war Jordan had been importing 55,000 barrels of oil a day from Iraq at a fixed price of US$16.40 which was below the market rate. As Saudi Arabia cut off supplies to Jordan in September 1990, Iraq was the country's only source of supply.

It seemed at the time that permanent damage might be inflicted on Jordan's political reforms especially in the light of a UNICEF study which revealed that the proportion of Jordanians living below the poverty line had risen from 20 per cent before the crisis, to 30 per cent after the conflict. Yet such fears were premature for in June 1991, King Hussein and representatives of the country's main political movements endorsed the national charter and accordingly lifted the ban on political parties in return for allegiance to the monarchy. The King reminded the country that political pluralism remained the only guarantee against dictatorship, adding that 'there is not a single party that can claim to possess the truth'.[30]

Conclusion

There can be no doubt that the obstacles facing democratizing policies in Jordan are considerable: rising indebtedness; increasing unemployment and potential polarization on the political front. With the Palestinian issue still unresolved in political, territorial and demographic terms the future is uncertain. Between 250,000 and 300,000 Palestinians have returned to Jordan from Kuwait placing a further strain on both the economy and political system and Arafat and the PLO continue to maintain close links with Saddam Hussein. In January 1992, Arafat wished the President of Iraq and his 'esteemed government, good health and happiness' on the basis that the 'pan-Arab stance of sisterly Iraq, its steadfast people and their leadership strongly supports the just cause of our people and their heroic national resistance'.[31] Precisely what the implications of this continuing friendship will mean to the Palestinians living in Jordan remains to be seen especially in the light of the about-turn in American foreign policy towards Jordan. King Hussein in November 1991, received General Joseph Hoar, Commander of the United States Central Command and his delegation to discuss 'general regional developments and arming and training matters geared to streamlining the armed forces'.[32] Whatever condemnations were made during the Gulf War it would seem that relations between the United States and Jordan are quite cordial.

But what have been the important features in Jordan's moves towards democratization and does its experience place it within a Third World model of political experiment? Certainly, Jordan's colonial background and poor economic status have parallels in other developing states but the crucial determining factor in Jordan's political system was the role played by population movement. The Palestinian factor was no mere transient problem but a deeply troubling, acute difficulty which penetrated every sphere of political and economic life. This is not simply a question of corrupt governments and impoverished leadership harnessing a country to authoritarian forms of political rule. This is a case of a majority of people who lived in one country and dreamed, desired, fought and eventually achieved legitimate leadership for their life in another. This was not a problem of development in the classic Third World mode, but a searing element which would have destabilized any advanced polity. Population movement and citizenship cuts to the very core the essential nature of nation-statehood and majority/minority apportionment is vital in sustaining a democracy.

If there are difficulties with citizenship and suspected affinities and loyalties these fears will be reflected in the political arena. It was perhaps inevitable that Jordan would have long periods with no elections and proscribed political parties; rule by decree and clamp-downs on a number of freedoms. Yet irrespective of the imbalance within the population, people did demonstrate for greater democratization and a return of political and civil rights. These demands take us to the second important factor within Jordan's attempts to liberalize: the indigenous push for democratization. When the IMF's restructuring scheme began to bite economically popular demonstrations made it quite clear that Jordanians were tired of political repression and wanted a change. But this move could not have taken place so effectively, or indeed, the King could not have felt the need to shift so quickly, had there not been a groundswell of political activity within Jordan for many years. Although there had been few elections and virtually no conduit for legitimate political opposition this does not completely extinguish political awareness and interest. As the 1989 elections reveal, once given the opportunity the electorate could exercise a level of autonomy and form associations with a variety of different groupings, thus utilizing their votes to maximum effect even within the obvious constraints.

However, indigenous movements must be balanced with another important factor: external pressure either of an international or regional variety. Within this broad category fall a number of variables: the Cold War, the

Arab-Israeli dispute, and the 1991 Gulf War all of which had an impact on Jordan's political system. The country's so-called Western orientation always placed it in a sensitive position *vis-à-vis* its pro-Soviet neighbours, consequently exacerbating regional tension. The Arab-Israeli dispute was always problematic, yet attempts at peace initiatives sometimes had a surprisingly beneficial effect as witnessed by the re-introduction of elections in the early 1980s. It definitely would appear that if some settlement could be found for the Arab-Israeli conflict, political pressure would diminish from that quarter. The Gulf War, on the other hand, at first sight appeared to undermine the prospects for reform but subsequently, its effects might not be so deleterious. Within the ambit of external influence, the role of the United States and its policy within the region is not exactly clear. However, two fundamental developments have taken place very recently which have the potential to create an environment more receptive to the establishment of democratic practices. First, the ending of the Cold War has clearly removed an important dynamic in the region and, second, the on-going international Middle East talks which began in Madrid a few months after the end of the Gulf War, create a modicum of hope that a settlement of the Palestinian-Israeli issue may be in view. If King Hussein, speaking in December 1991 is right democracy, far from being destabilizing and potentially threatening may 'now be a guarantee of security and stability'.[29]

Kuwait

Kuwait's existence at the geographic head of the Gulf, bordering Iraq and Saudi Arabia, has perenially been controlled, claimed or challenged. In fact, it has not been regarded as a nation state: 'Kuwait is not a country, not a people, not a city, not even a town. It is an oil oasis'.[33] One thing it certainly has, however, is a powerful ruling family; the Al-Sabah family has been dominant since the eighteenth century. Kuwait was under British protectorate status since 1899 in order to protect it from interference from the Ottoman Empire and did not gain full independence until 1961. Immediately Kuwait announced its independence, Iraq renewed its claims to sovereignty over the country claiming that during the Ottoman period it formed part of the Basra province. No other Arab country supported Iraq's claims, and in July 1961, the Arab League admitted Kuwait as a full member state. In 1963 Kuwait became a member of the United Nations and although later that year Iraq recognized the country's independence it still laid territorial claims to the Kuwaiti islands of Warbah and Bubiyan. In a sense, then, Kuwait has been troubled by questions of identity and, to a degree, regional legitimacy.

Al-Sabah Family/Constitution 1962

In December 1961, for the first time in Kuwaiti history, an election was held to choose members of the Constituent Assembly. The Assembly drafted a new constitution, inaugurated in 1962 under Amir Abdullah al Salim Al Salim, the head of a prominent merchant family who had settled in Kuwait in the eighteenth century. The Constitution provided for the establishment of a legislature, the National Assembly and an executive body, the Council of Ministers. Ultimate authority, of course, rested with the Amir but Michael Hudson suggests that the Kuwaiti structure of government could be termed a 'liberal-nationalist model', characterized by a combination of 'benevolent personal rule, representative structures and nationalist ideology'.[34] Yet a leading oppositionist to the Al-Sabah form of rule raises a note of caution and maintains that the ruling family always disliked the 1962 constitution, seeing it as a threat to their authority, and consequently, were determined to undermine it.[35]

The fundamental difficulty with the constitution is that while offering formal structures of participation it provided little democratic content and certainly did not reflect the demographic balance of the country. The role of the Al-Sabah family is not the only obstacle to meaningful participation. As mentioned in the previous chapter, one central problem within the country is the configuration of the population and the implications it holds for electoral enfranchisement. Although Kuwait is the only Gulf state with a national assembly elected entirely by popular vote, a closer inspection exposes its frailties. A population estimate on 1 August 1990, amounted to 2 million persons, of whom approximately 70 per cent were non-Kuwaitis.[36] Suffrage, however, is confined to male citizens over 21 years of age who can prove Kuwaiti ancestry prior to 1920. At the time of the 1981 elections it was estimated that these eligibile voters comprised only 6.4 per cent of the total population.[37] It can be seen, therefore, that the term 'popular vote' is something of a misnomer and within this context, the notion of 'representative structures' can be very misleading.

Nevertheless, even within such a severely circumscribed electoral system, opposition was exercised against the government during those early post-independent years. Supporters of the Democratic National Alliance, an organization led by Dr Ahmed Al-Khatib, could be elected and in the absence of political parties this group was generally regarded as the principal opposition to the government. After the elections of 1971, the Cabinet included two ministers drawn from the elected members of the National Assembly which, after 1975 increased to include seven new ministers. These moves, however, proved too much for the Amir who promptly dissolved parliament in 1976 and ordered the creation of a committee to review the 1962 constitution.

Oil and politics

Political changes within Kuwait during the 1970s must be seen against the backdrop of Iraq's aggrandizement in 1973 and the massive oil price rise of the same period. In March 1973, Iraqi troops and tanks occupied a Kuwaiti outpost at Samitah on the border and a military clash ensued. Iraq eventually withdrew in 1974. During the Arab-Israeli war of October 1973, Kuwait called for a meeting of the Organization of Arab Petroleum Exporting Countries (OAPEC) in order that a common Arab policy could be drawn up with the purpose of using oil as a weapon to put pressure on Western countries to enforce an Israeli withdrawal from the West Bank and Gaza. Kuwait, along with other Gulf States announced an increase of 70 per cent in the price of crude petroleum with effect from 1 November 1973. It was also agreed that oil production would fall by 25 per cent. Kuwait played a leading role in these moves and the government decided to take over the Kuwait National Petroleum Company, in which it already had a 60 per cent share.

The oil price hike of the 1970s set Kuwait and the other oil rich states apart from other nations in the Third World. It seemed that those oil rich countries had moved into 'easy street' leaving the detritus of economic malfunction and political instability to the poorer nations. Yet it would seem paradoxical that as oil price rises created tensions within developing countries, ultimately contributing to a spiralling Third World debt crisis, simultaneously, in the wake of such increases in oil wealth, certain Arab states became more politically repressive. The dissolution of the National Assembly in Kuwait in 1976 should be viewed in this context. The political environment of Kuwait had a deep and lasting impact on the management of its strategic national interests, that is, oil. In essence, oil resources fell under the political and economic control of a small elite with the result that an unaccountable government could proceed to run its oil industries almost as personal fiefdoms. It was one thing for the Amir and Crown Prince to publicly affirm the government's intention to restore the National Assembly and return to some semblance of democratic government, but in actuality it took five years to re-introduce elections. Even when the elections did take place in February 1981, of those 'first class' Kuwaitis eligible to vote less than half registered which amounted to around 3 per cent of the total population. Not surprisingly, a moderate assembly was returned containing 23 Conservative tribal leaders sympathetic to the ruling family, and the Al-Sabah family retained the key posts in the new 15-member Cabinet. These features of Kuwait's political system taken together with the government's introduction of wide-ranging welfare benefits have contributed to the view that the country perfectly fits the model of the 'rentier state'.

The 'rentier state'

The absence of full democratic involvement within Kuwait is considered by some social scientists to be closely associated with the country's dependency on oil revenues, which accumulate in the form of 'rent'. In a 'rentier state' revenue is derived from external rather than domestic sources; it accrues directly to the state and as a consequence of this process the state becomes distanced from society. There is no requirement to tax citizens and without taxation there is unlikely to be representation. The citizenry of such states are not engaged in productive activity and, therefore, have no need to form trade unions or political parties, or, indeed, any organization charged with an economic imperative. Their needs are met by the State's distribution of goods and services, that is, its allocation of oil wealth, in the form of welfarism. The State's central function, therefore, is an allocative one.

The assumption is made that only when a state relies on taxation will the question of democracy become an 'unavoidable issue'. Luciani asserts that democracy is not a problem for allocation states:

> Although they may find it expedient to set up some kind of representative body to vent and control some of the resentment that every court politics generates, these bodies inevitably have a very tenuous link to their constituency: their debates are followed by indifference by the public and the ruler can disband them and meet practically no resistance whatsoever.[38]

Opposition in such a country as Kuwait, then, would only manifest itself if the state was no longer able to maintain revenue levels or became subservient to a foreign power. With such an inextricable link forged between economic productive forces and the emergence of democracy it could be possible to consider Kuwait to be a completely lost case, although practitioners and supporters of the Democratic National Alliance might not agree with such a conclusion. Dr al-Khatib and other oppositionist groups were jailed for demanding the re-institution of the National Assembly and defending minimal political rights.

The 1985 elections for the National Assembly resulted in the return of the Democratic National Alliance again headed by Dr Ahmed Al-Khatib. The Alliance stood on a reformist, pan-Arab and pro-Palestinian platform and during the campaign touched a raw nerve when it criticized the extent to which Kuwait's oil revenues were being invested in the United States. The deputies in that newly elected Assembly, far from simply 'venting their resentment', presented the government with formidable opposition which was amplified by the press. The cabinet witnessed government bills being rejected and the resignation of the Justice Minister. The Assembly had changed from being a consultative body tamed by a dominant government, to a more assertive, demanding entity. Ironically, it was this strength which led to parliament being suspended in July 1986; an action which, of course, could be construed as fitting a 'rentier state' analysis. There is no doubt that following the enormous increases in oil revenue accruing to the government, the Amir and his entourage became more sensitive to criticism and consequently, more repressive. The political stakes, obviously, were much higher, particularly as the Assembly was endeavouring to investigate financial corruption in the Al-Sabah family.[39]

Along with dissolving the only elected parliament in the Gulf region, the Amir imposed censorship on the press, re-appointed the Crown Prince as Prime Minister, and suspended Article 107 of the Constitution which stipulated that elections must be held within two months of the dissolution of the National Assembly. The Amir, at will, had completely transformed the political environment of the country. He had demonstrated comprehensively the extent and range of his power. However, and this is the significant point, the exercise of that authority had resulted in considerable resistance which ultimately culminated in the imprisonment of leaders of opposition groups. The Amir viewed criticism of the government by the elected deputies as an abuse of a democratic institution: 'I saw a shaken democracy in front of me', he maintained, 'and with it the society and unity of the country was shaken so it became my responsibility to dissolve parliament'.[40] The Amir had rather missed the point about democracy. The role of parliament was not to serve as a supportive group to the Al-Sabah family but to question, examine and oppose the government if it felt the necessity to do so. In his dissolution speech the Amir stated that he still believed in the principle of 'parliamentary consultation'.[41] The term 'parliamentary consultation' reveals a rather different interpretation of the role of a national assembly to that understood in the West; accountability and criticism are not included, merely debate and discussion in the classic 'Shura' tradition. However, the point at issue here is not that the Amir could and, indeed, did dissolve parliament but that his traditionalist views were not held by other Kuwaitis and he was obliged to brook opposition for some considerable time.

Pressures to liberalize

In 1989, three years after the dissolution of the National Assembly, reports indicated that senior officials within Kuwait had been involved in the circulation of secret petitions calling for a return to parliamentary life. It was believed at the time that between 30,000 and 40,000 Sunni Muslims had signed the petitions.[42] Also between December 1989 and January 1990 a series of unprecedented pro-democracy street rallies took place which allegedly forced the government to call an election for June 1990.[43] It is difficult to pinpoint the catalyst for these quite radical moves. Certainly, in a country where 70 per cent of the population are semi-citizens or non-citizens there is likely to be some level of political uneasiness. This factor was evident during the Iran–Iraq war in the 1980s. Although Kuwaitis dismissed the possibility of internal subversion by Shi'ite terrorist groups, a community which formed a significant 30 per cent of Kuwait's population, the ad-Dawa al-Islamiya (the Voice of Islam) organization attempted to assassinate the Amir in 1985. Resulting from this attack greater security measures were introduced and controls over entry visas and resident permits were introduced. It may have been the increased security measures which acted as an instigator of the demands for reform.

The elections which were held in June 1990 were surrounded by controversy. According to official figures 62,000 people voted to elect 50 members to a new National Assembly. A further 25 seats were to be directly appointed by the Amir. The elections fell short of the demands for the full restoration of parliament. Although it was claimed that 503 candidates had taken part, the full results were not released. Charges were made that the electoral rolls had been interfered with and that people had been pressurized to vote, or refused a vote or, indeed, discovered that someone had voted in their place. Certainly, opposition groups had campaigned for a boycott of the elections on the grounds that they were unconstitutional and that the power of parliament, such as it was, would be further constrained. Press censorship continued and opposition leaders were arrested for addressing illegal meetings. It was quite clear that although the Amir held control of the apparatus of power he could not stem the demands for some form of representative government. It might be possible to govern a country in which police forces are employed to disperse meetings with tear gas and baton charges in attempts to eliminate opposition; brute force has always been a potent element, but those actions cannot deny the existence of progressive movements.[44] In essence, then, on the eve of the invasion of the country by Iraq, Kuwait's political system was hardly a showpiece of democracy. However, the Al-Sabah family would soon realize that the country's demographic balance which was reinforced by the state's harsh naturalization laws possessed political and security problems for the nation. Also, Kuwait's political structures would soon receive the glare of international attention.

The Gulf War 1991

On 2 August 1990 Kuwait was invaded by Iraq. During the crisis, as is perhaps inevitable, opposition groups, including the Democratic National Alliance, united with the Amir in the belief there should be a return to constitutional government after the conflict. According to Dr al-Khatib's statement in May 1991, three months after the Gulf War and the withdrawal of Iraqi troops from the country, all Kuwaiti citizens, including the Armed Forces and the secret services supported the institution of a form of democracy.[45] These sentiments seemed genuine for in April 1991, six main opposition parties, including both secular and Islamic groups signed a manifesto demanding a free press, an independent judiciary, legalized political parties and anti-corruption measures. The Amir, himself, in his first major speech since returning from self-imposed exile during the war, announced that elections to a new parliament would be held in 1992. He promised to study the question of women's participation in parliamentary life and hinted that the status of naturalized 'second category' citizens, previously denied the vote would be reviewed.[46]

Given that all attention was focused on Kuwait, a war had just been fought under the sanction of the United Nations and preparations were being made for a defence pact to be signed between Kuwait and the United States, it might not be unreasonable to deduce that external pressure might have caused the Amir's dramatic change of heart. Viewed from this perspective it should have come as no surprise that the high hopes of a radical political change would meet with disappointment when the Amir named the members of the new government, which although including a number of technocrats, did not embrace any members of the opposition movements. The new cabinet, according to oppositionists, represented a challenge to popular opinion especially in the light of the fact that discussions had taken place just a matter of weeks previously, regarding the formation of a more representative government including a coalition of merchant groups, Islamic parties and former members of parliament. Then, in May 1991, just a month after these meetings, five members of the Islamic Constitutional Movement were arrested which further confirmed uncertainty and doubts about the possibilities of political reform. The decree issued by the Amir in June ordering elections to a new national assembly to be held in October 1992, failed to quell doubts that the government was simply prevaricating. Opposition politicians denounced the decree as a facade of democracy and an estimated 1000 people attended an opposition rally to demand the immediate restoration of democracy.[47]

It was clear that external pressure could only accomplish limited goals in pursuit of the democratization of Kuwait. The demographic factor was the key to any sustainable move towards reforming the country. The government recognized that it was vital that Kuwait reshape its population to make Kuwaitis a majority, and this it intended to achieve by a reduction in overall population. Palestinians had, of course, fled the country following their support of Iraq during the conflict and the government acknowledged that the demographic question concerned the country's security. Arguably, had Kuwaitis not been a minority in their own country, Saddam Hussein might not have invaded. Citizenship, rights and responsibilities have as much to do with the defence of a nation as they have with the maintenance of representative institutions. To deny people who have been resident in a land for decades the appropriate status is to undermine the fabric of a nation-state and render it vulnerable both internally and externally.

Conclusion

Kuwait, without its oil wealth, would probably be regarded as an impoverished Third World country with an authoritarian and autocratic leader not dissimilar to any number of states in Africa and Asia who gained independence in the 1960s. The attempts and associated failures to introduce democratic practices in the country could be explained by problems of unity, nation-building and probably even the unsuitability of introducing potentially divisive and destabilizing democratic forms of government to such a polity. Kuwait, without its enormous gross national product, might be excused its political failings. But Kuwait presents a paradox; it has both vast wealth and a repressive, unrepresentative form of rule. As an explanation for this situation, the 'rentier state' analysis offers a sophisticated interpretation of the relationship between economic forces and political reform and at first sight the model appears to fit Kuwait perfectly. The image of the paternalistic ruler, dispensing welfare in a benevolent state and thus buying off any demands for political liberalization seems an apt picture of Kuwait's political system. Some analysts supported the view. According to Michael Hudson writing in the late 1970s, apart from 'occasional stirrings of resentment at the family's monopoly of power, there has been no serious challenge'.[48] The reason for this rested with the Amir's 'competence and custom'.

However, events in the more recent past present a rather different view of political behaviour in Kuwait. The Amir's increasing tendency to dissolve the National Assembly and rule by decree; the shift away from constitutional modes of conduct; the recourse to imprisonment for leading oppositionist figures; the secret petitions calling for a return to representative government; the demonstrations in the streets raising pleas for greater democratization and accountability, all point to an increasingly uneasy domestic political environment, unpacified by welfare packages. Add to this, the threat of regional tension and belligerency and a picture emerges of a ruling family, far from comfortable and inviolable in its charitable dispensations of oil wealth, and under challenge. Consequently, when considering Kuwait's political structures from this viewpoint the 'rentier state' model seems less appropriate. Clearly, there are democratic currents running through the country which could be explained by the fact that democratization can, at times, follow an incrementalist pattern. When Kuwait became independent the 1962 Constitution set down certain guidelines which would facilitate political participation: elections for the selected few, a national assembly and so on. Whatever the deficiencies of those processes they did represent a definite move in a liberalizing direction and they exposed an element of the population, albeit a minute section, to a certain degree of political participation. In common with other developing states when even small democratic concessions have been granted and then subsequently withdrawn, the Kuwaiti leadership finds itself in the parlous position of actually creating and fomenting political opposition. It is quite natural for people to object when political rights are taken from them; it is after all, part of the struggle of historical political reform that people resist the removal of their rights. Inevitably, such resistance has occurred in Kuwait.

The interesting feature about Kuwait, however, and one which it shares with Jordan, is its demographic composition. There is no question that such a large imbalance which renders the indigenous population a minority in its own country is profoundly problematic. The migrant labour employed in Kuwait whilst on the one hand providing a source of economic sustenance to countries like Jordan, forming in a sense, the other side of Jordan's demographic coin, always carried the potential to undermine the state. Any political reform in Kuwait must seriously confront the dual questions of citizenship and political rights, otherwise democratization will be be retarded. This brings us to the question of external pressure, especially the role which the United States appears to have adopted. According to reports in July 1992, the National Republican Institute for International Affairs, an organization affiliated to the US Republican Party has been promoting the introduction of democratization in Kuwait.[49] Certainly, this pressure helps to account for the Amir's reformist speeches after the Gulf War, but in the final analysis, the prospects for democratization will largely depend on how Kuwait copes with its population problem.

So what can we learn from the examples of the political systems of Jordan and Kuwait? One conclusion is absolutely certain: there is an inextricable relationship between citizenship and the functions of the state. Any difficulty with citizenship will inevitably have an impact in the political arena and will inhibit reform, irrespective of the economic base of the country. The issue, of course, is not confined to Third World polities but has a far wider global significance. If the indigenous population of a given country, for whatever reason, finds itself in a minority, political repression may, indeed, follow. In this sense both the Amir in Kuwait and King Hussein in Jordan are under pressure both externally and internally to liberalize their political systems and the time now may seem propitious for such moves. However, if democratization is to continue in any meaningful way, basic questions of citizenship must be addressed in both countries.

The theocratic state – Iran

Iran, a Persian and not an Arab state, once possessed a wide-ranging empire which competed at times with Arab spheres of interest. The country's pedigree is important for its non-Arab status raises interesting questions. The features of 'Arabness', that is: common language, culture, religion, race, etc., the so-called 'primordial loyalties' which allegedly serve to bind peoples in the Middle East within the 'Arab Nation' at the expense of nation-statehood, do not embrace the region as a whole. Clearly, what might be offered as an explanation of one form of political system, in terms of Arab culture and predisposition, manifested in, for example, a nation's belligerency towards another state, the way it conducted its affairs, its recourse to repression, the role played by religion and the extent to which political reforms had been introduced, would not seem to be applicable in a non-Arab state. At first sight, it might appear that Arab and non-Arab states have little in common. Iran was not the artificial construction of imperialist command, it was not the subject of formal colonial control, and it possessed a distinctive cultural history and set of traditions. Yet features of Iranian political life resemble those of other nations in the region. The examples of repression, dislocated elections, proscribed parties, authoritarian rule, ideological competition and the rise in the political significance of religion, can be replicated in the polities of most of Iran's neighbouring Arab states. This tendency would suggest that certain conditions existed over and above those of 'primordial loyalties' and have affected Iran along with other states in the area. This chapter identifies those common factors to be the prominence of external influences and more importantly the Cold War, and the indigenous development and polarization of ideological currents of thought and political parties.

However, other themes will also be addressed. First, the extent to which the rise of Islam was perceived to be a beneficial alternative to Iran's existing political structure. It must be acknowledged, after all, that the revolution received considerable support from left-wing quarters and those traditionally associated with the political centre-ground. Second, the nature of the Theocratic state as constitutionally defined at the time of the revolution in 1979. Third, the degree to which the renewed emphasis on political participation within the country, provides a real democratic option for the Iranian polity within an Islamic state. In essence, is there an Islamic model of democracy operating within Iran?

External influences

Although Iran did not fall under formal colonial rule, it was, during the Second World War, occupied by British, American and Soviet troops because of its German sympathies. This occupation was divisive for whilst the Iranian Communist Tudeh Party was encouraged in the northern Soviet controlled territory, Britain owned the country's most important asset, the Anglo-Iranian Oil Company. Thus, in the early 1950s one of the key themes echoing through Iran, in common with many post-colonial nations, was the need for the country to free itself from foreign domination and influence, and the most obvious way for the country to assert its own authority would be to nationalize the Anglo-Iranian Oil Company.

At that time the country had a legislative assembly, the Majlis, and an executive body, led by the Prime Minister, Mohammed Mossadeq, who presided over a coalition of national groups, united under the umbrella title, the National Front. The majlis was a traditional feature of Iranian political culture and indeed in the 1906 constitution a clause included a process of judicial review of parliamentary legislation to be carried out by the Shi'i 'ulama, or mullahs. The rationale of the Majlis was to curb the power of the ruler, who since 1941, was Mohammed Reza Shah. Consequently, any policy of nationalization of the Anglo-Iranian Oil Company, would need the approval of the majlis, which it in fact received. Britain was outraged and immediately instituted a boycott of Iranian oil which created a profound economic crisis. The Shah with the assistance of the British Intelligence services and the American Central Intelligence Agency organized a coup d'état to replace Mossadeq with a military government. This action may well have been considered appropriate by Britain and the United States but it was to create a groundswell of anti-Western opinion which would fester in the years to come. With the Shah firmly in power and a military government established, the United States announced the donation of a US$23.4 million grant for technical and military projects, together with aid of US$45 million.[1]

The six-year period of military rule between 1953 and 1959 witnessed the curtailment of the press and a general clamp-down on political activities. Although the Tudeh Party was the most severely suppressed with its leaders imprisoned or executed, the National Front did not escape punishment. Most of its leaders were also imprisoned and in this atmosphere, the National Resistance Movement (NRM) a loose, clandestine coalition of former National Front members emerged in late 1954. This organization was interesting in that it combined religious and secular nationalists. However, although the organization united disparate elements, they were divided on strategy for whilst religious figures considered the military regime to be illegitimate, secular leaders were prepared to operate through legal channels. This approach was completely unworkable and eventually all the leaders of the NRM were arrested. Perhaps, the NRM's greatest weakness was its inability to unite on a programme of reform although, of course, in mitigation, it was operating in oppressive times and scarcely had time to formulate one. One of the recurring features of political associations during Iran's period of authoritarian rule under the Shah was their inability to provide a real political alternative. The fact that Ayatollah Khomeini did precisely that in the late 1970s was Islam's real strength.

The Cold War

In 1959 a bilateral defence agreement was signed between Iran and the United States under the aegis of the 'Eisenhower Doctrine', in which it was agreed that the USA 'will in the case of aggression, take such appropriate action, including the use of armed force, as may be mutually agreed to promote peace and security in the Middle East'.[2] If this reassured the Americans that their interests were secure in Iran it had two impacts on Iranian politics. First, the Shah was regarded as a 'puppet' of the United States thus increasing anti-Western sentiment; second, the Shah felt enhanced by his relationship with America and consequently, was resistant to the emergence of any candidate whom the US might possibly 'be inclined to support in preference to himself'.[3] As a result, he was compelled to follow increasingly repressive measures not only against leftist opposition but also against the centre. As C. D. Carr asserts, 'When the Shah finally fell from power there did not exist any group or individual with the experience or training capable of representing the middle ground in Iranian politics.'[4]

In 1957 a new Prime Minister was appointed who announced his intention of ending martial law and establishing a democratic two-party system, in accordance with the wishes of the Shah. The purpose of this policy change was to create the impression of a functioning pluralistic democracy. There are various interpretations as to why this shift of position took place.

One view points to American influence which propelled Iran to forge some kind of political reform and one is reminded of Samuel Huntington's views on the importance of America assisting certain countries in the development of political parties, which interestingly was written at the same period.[5] An alternative argument maintains that the US had little influence and points to a State Department report which recorded the question of ordering Iran to establish genuine democratic institutions: 'These suggestions presuppose that the Shah is a creature of the US . . . a common misperception in Iran. Any US ultimatums or even heavy-handed hints would be regarded by the Shah as an intolerable interference in his affairs and would probably result in corresponding moves on his part towards the USSR.'[6] However, when elections did take place in 1960 they were unquestionably fraudulent. The Shah had personally chosen the candidates of the two bespoke parties, the Nation Party and the People's Party, who readily admitted they were competing in the elections only to please the Shah. Ultimately, the elections had to be annulled because of accusations of irregularities and ballot rigging. However, the new elections held in January 1961 were again contested by Iran's only two legal parties. Supporters of the National Front claimed these elections were also rigged and in response to these protests, the National Front's headquarters were closed. By May the Shah had dissolved parliament announcing that 'elections at the present time are too risky.'[7] Demonstrations took place in Tehran, police opened fire, killing several people. Opposition was voiced by a clergyman, Khomeini, who claimed that the Shah had violated the constitution by failing to call new elections within a month of the dissolution of parliament.

The existence of the Communist Tudeh Party in Iran always complicated the political scene; against the background of the Cold War, it was looked upon as a potentially subversive organization. It also served as a constant reminder to the United States of the possible threat to its interests from the Soviet Union and at times served to justify the Shah's repressive measures. To be simply a democrat in the Shah's period implied marginalization, especially in the 1970s when two pincer movements were squeezing Iranian society like a lemon. One arm of the pincer US President Nixon's 'Twin Pillar' policy towards Iran, specifying that Iran's military capacity was to be built up in order for it to become the undisputed military power in the Gulf and, along with Saudi Arabia, protect American interests in the region. The second development was the increasing dominance and extended sphere of interests of SAVAK. In 1975, the Shah formally announced the formation of a single-party system, under the newly formed 'Iran National Resurgence Party (Rastakhiz). There would be no political opposition of any form and SAVAK's role was to eliminate any organization or group considered to be a threat to the regime, in other words all organizations.

Ghods maintains that it was the Shah's political and military ties with the United States which facilitated the build-up of his police state.[8] Certainly, the Shah could do no wrong in the eyes of President Nixon who referred to him as a 'world statesman of the first rank'.[9] Also, more importantly, the sophisticated weaponry which America was supplying to Iran was provided in exchange for an increased US quota of Iranian oil. This arrangement made sense from both the United States' and the Shah's points of view, particularly after the oil price rises of 1973/74, but suspicions surfaced that America was turning a blind eye to the Shah's repressive measures. The inconsistencies of US policy on the one hand championing human rights whilst on the other, ignoring Iran's abuse of such rights, did not go unnoticed and further fomented anti-Western opinion.

The White Revolution

In 1963 the Shah instituted the so-called White Revolution and a number of reforming measures were proclaimed including the redistribution of land among the peasantry; the emancipation of women and improved literacy programmes. According to new electoral laws the franchise would be extended to every Iranian, male or female over the age of 20. This was a radical change from previous electoral stipulations in which voters and candidates had to be male, Muslim and swear an oath by the Qur'an. The clergy viewed this move as a direct challenge to Shi'ism and the reform allegedly marked a turning point in the Shah's relationship with the clergy.[10] The Shah had little time for religious leaders and in a speech in the holy city of Qom, referred to the clergy as 'always a stupid and reactionary bunch whose brains have not moved' and accused them of being 'one hundred times more treacherous than the Tudeh Party'.[11]

The Shah was in a difficult position, he had offended the clergy but he had also alienated support from the National Front for what were essentially reformist and liberalizing measures, on the grounds that they did not bring substantial political benefits. The National Front's slogan at the time was 'Reforms Yes, Dictatorship No'.[12] It was quite possible to tamper with electoral laws and make them appear more democratic when in reality, elections were something of a farce and meaningful political parties were suppressed or proscribed. The White Revolution's policies provided the Shah with an image of modernity yet no real political participation was envisaged and certainly no political competition or opposition was permitted. In short, it was business as usual with the Shah completely in command of the apparatus of power.

However, the proposed land reforms helped to create a new bourgeoisie whose political aspirations required channels of participation. By refusing to parallel economic reforms with political development, the Shah blocked those potential conduits and created deep resentment and distrust amongst the newly emerging middle classes. It is not surprising that Islam became a focus for resistance. In the 1970s an organization called the Mujahedin-e-Khalq (Holy Warriors of the People) a guerrilla group combining Islam with armed struggle, was formed. The Mujahedin advocated the creation of a people's army who would engage in attacks on the regime. Even the outlawed Tudeh Party regained support as a result of its recognition of religion as a basis for political opposition: 'We accept militant religion as a force to fight against oppression and injustice; we do not accept it as a force that teaches ignorance, passivity, mysticism, and self pity.'[13] The Shah had created the conditions for increasing political polarization at the expense of the middle ground. As demonstrations and political violence began to build up in 1977 and 1978 it seemed inevitable that a dramatic change would occur.

The revolution

Whenever an authoritarian leader feels threatened by forces he senses are becoming out of his control, last-ditch attempts are made at introducing political reforms. The Shah introduced just such a policy when in early 1979, the former deputy leader of the National Front, Shapour Bakhtiar was charged with forming a 'last-chance' government. Bakhtiar's acceptance of the position resulted in his immediate expulsion from the National Front movement on the grounds of his 'betrayal'.[14] His willingness to become Premier at the behest of the Shah was judged to be opportunistic even though he had previously served prison sentences totalling five years for activities against the Shah. The Bakhtiar government was destined to have a limited life-span for it included no members of secular or religious opposition groups. It was also vulnerable to potential misuse by the Shah despite his proclaimed wish to leave the country, and to disruption by either Ayatollah Khomeini's Islamic Republican Party or the National Front. Although Bakhtiar's reforms were radical – the dissolution of SAVAK; release of political prisoners; lifting of press censorship; legalization of parties and a greater role for Muslim clerics in the drafting of legislation – there was no certainty as to precisely how genuine these policies were likely to be, especially as it was unclear whether or not the Shah was actually leaving for good or, as Bakhtiar stated, simply going away 'for a period of rest and holiday'.[15]

Three days before the Shah's departure on 16 January 1979, a nine-man Regency Council was formed under the chairmanship of Sayed Jalal Tehrani, a former cabinet minister and loyal supporter of the Shah. The members included Dr Bakhtiar; the new Chief of Staff, General Abbas Qharabaghi; and the chairman of the National Iranian Oil Company; hardly a group likely to inspire confidence in the nation at large. The Council was formed under Article 42 of the Constitution which provided for the temporary departure of the Shah from the country. It was empowered to dissolve parliament, call elections or establish a constituent assembly to bring about a possible transition to a new regime. However, on the day the Regency Council was formed, Ayatollah Khomeini announced the creation of a 'Revolutionary Islamic Council' which would allegedly replace the 'illegal government' and set up a provisional Islamic government to oversee elections to a constituent assembly. Khomeini was living in exile in Paris at the time and one of the leaders of the National Front, Dr Mehdi Bazargan, attempted to mediate between the Ayatollah and the government in an attempt to reach a compromise agreement on the transition to a new administration, but to no avail.

The Shah left Iran on 16 January 1979 and tumultuous celebrations took place in major towns and cities. Khomeini returned to Iran on 1 February and was greeted by thousands of supporters. Critics, of course, have pointed to the public euphoria which greeted Khomeini's rise to power as evidence of a strong authoritarian streak indelibly stamped through Iranian society which was antithetical to the development of democratic institutions.[16] Others judged Iranian political factionalism in which 'ideological and personal differences made co-operation between and within secular parties next to impossible', as being the fundamentally weak link in the country's political development.[17] Certainly, Khomeini attracted considerable support from a variety of political quarters. He appointed Mehdi Bazargan as Prime Minister of his provisional government. Bazargan had served in the ill-fated Mossadeq government and subsequently was imprisoned and had founded the National Resistance Movement, a centrist group, which affiliated to the National Front in 1962. Two well-known National Front leaders, Dariush Foruhar and Karim Sanjabi were also included in Bazargan's cabinet. As the tide of popular support for Khomeini rose, support and assistance was forthcoming from the Mujahedin-e-Khalq, the far left, Cherik Fedayeen-e Khalq and the Communist Tudeh Party. Yet it must be stated that the new regime seemed to achieve a degree of constitutional legitimacy in a country which had a tradition of Islamic political activity. Historically, the Shi'a mullahs had played a distinctive political role which has been attributed to their 'tight hierarchical organization' permitting a high level of cohesion. Accordingly, religious leaders had exercised successful resistance against the former autocracy of the Qajar dynasty as far back as the 1890s.[18] Also, Ayatollah Khomeini had deemed it necessary to form a political party, the Islamic Republican Party in 1978, with the intention of instituting an Islamic revolution and that party was subsequently disbanded in 1987.

In March 1979, a referendum was held, in which voters were asked 'Are you for the replacement of the monarchy by an Islamic Republic, the constitution of which will be approved – yes or no?'[19] Both the National Front and the Tudeh Party supported a yes vote. Once again Khomeini utilized an ostensibly democratic feature to legitimize the regime in the eyes both of the population and other political parties. The official results of the referendum revealed that of the 20,288,021 votes cast only 140,966 had voted against, although two factors were to militate against this result. First, the ballot was not secret in that voters were obliged to produce identity documents; and second, they were provided with no real choice. As Matine-Daftari, grandson of Mossadeq, commented: 'It was anti-democratic to expect people to choose between a government which they had themselves overthrown and a system of government as yet unknown.'[20] Of course, this view is absolutely right but given that the population was emerging from an excessively repressive period, even to be permitted to participate in such a process was taken as a sign that freedoms were returning and the political climate was changing. Clearly, the draft constitution, as it stood on 18 June 1979, seemed to represent a significant step in a democratic direction and a considerable break with the past. It contained provisions for a nationally elected president, a unicameral parliament and promised the establishment of an independent judiciary, full human rights and religious tolerance. Elections were held in August 1979 to a 73-member Constituent Council of Experts which would finalize the constitution. Although over 80 per cent of the 1000 candidates were clerics, the elections were also contested by the Mujahedin and Fedayeen movements and the Tudeh Party. The National Front were beginning to become uneasy and called for a boycott. However, in those early months of the revolution, characteristics associated with democratic behaviour were introduced to the Iranian polity: elections, a referendum, party pluralism and the possibilities of further liberties to be enshrined in a new Constitution. It was precisely those democratic features which proved to be so attractive to the public even when signs indicated their chimerical quality. When an amended constitution which essentially placed all power in the hands of one man: Ayatollah Khomeini was placed before the people at yet another referendum in December 1979, it was supported by 15,680,329 votes to 78,516.

The theocratic state

The principal amendments to the constitution made by the Constituent Council of Experts established the Shi'a branch of Islam as the country's official religion and, more importantly, gave supreme power to the preeminent Shi'a religious leader, the Wali Faqi. In the event of there being no generally recognized spiritual authority, the theologians' rule was to be exercised by a college of clerics. According to Article 94 all legislation passed by the 270-member Majlis, must be reviewed by the Council for the Protection of the Constitution where it is scrutinized for its Islamic content. The government of the Islamic Republic of Iran should embrace the spirituality and ethics of Islam and such elements should provide the basis for political, social and economic relations. The amended constitution provided for elections to the Majlis every four years and permitted the formation of political and professional parties, associations and societies so long as they did not negate the basis of Islam. Similarly, the press was intended to be free except in matters which were deemed contrary to public morality or insulting to religious belief. In reality, of course, the Constitution presented a series of contradictions which masked a variant of the one-party state.

During those early months of the Islamic Republic, Khomeini operated his Revolutionary Council and local Komitehs, or revolutionary committees and revolutionary courts were set up. A Revolutionary Guard combined the functions of an army, a police force and a mosque. Khomeini proclaimed the Revolutionary Council would take over the running of the country while preparing for elections to the Majlis and a national President. The elections resulted in the Islamic Republic Party and its supporters winning the majority of seats, but allegations of vote-rigging and interference so familiar during the Shah's rule now echoed within the new regime.

The somewhat peculiar alliance between the secular and religious groups which had united in order to overthrow the Shah found, not surprisingly, disagreements emerging. It was inevitable that Khomeini would denounce Marxism and atheism. Any association between Islamic fundamentalism and Marxist-Leninism was always suspect, and although the Mujahedin and the Tudeh Party had largely assisted in facilitating the revolution, when they had ceased to be useful, they were duly declared illegal. The Mujahedin engaged in armed action against the government but it resulted in their execution and a wave of repression. The Tudeh Party was proscribed in May 1983 and its leaders were arrested. It was reminiscent of old pre-revolutionary times for the party to be once again an outlawed movement, yet this time there was the bitter knowledge that by following the supposedly correct leftist strategy of uniting with oppositionist forces at a time of instability, the Tudeh Party had succeeded in conniving for the victory of a regime which if no worse than the Shah's, was certainly no better.

Through the introduction of the Islamic legal code, Sharia, it was possible rigorously to enforce Islamic ideas through a formal set of procedures and rules which applied to the penal system, judicial interpretation, strict dress and social laws. Hence, the state was enabled, via these instruments of control to 'forge a superficial homogeneity upon Iranian society'.[21] The Islamic state, therefore, serves to combine symbolism with authority.

Some analysts do not view the Islamic State as necessarily reactionary but rather as a post-modern phenomenon, thus: 'Islamic fundamentalism reflects the modernist ideas of secularism and a secular state and society, which are felt to have failed in providing an appropriate and moral social order for humans.'[22] The apparatus of the modern state is adapted to conform to religious imperatives but the nature of the repression required to stem opposition within the polity can be just as barbaric and arbitrary. There is, arguably, no difference between SAVAMA, the Islamic Republic's secret police and the former Shah's SAVAK, the State Organization for Intelligence and Security, on which it was modelled, in that both have instituted close systematic surveillance over the population. In short, then certain identifiable features have lingered on from the Shah's period and connect pre- and post-revolutionary Iran in what has been essentially a shift from one totalitarian phase to another. According to reports by both Amnesty International and the United Nations Human Rights Commission issued in December 1990, 5000 people were executed in Iran between 1987 and 1990. The reports also point to the fact that prisoners had no recourse to legal counsel or right of appeal.[23] This purge of oppositionists which included not only left-wing political activists and sympathizers, but also several clergymen was the result of a crack-down on all 'those who have betrayed Islam and the revolution'.[24] In 1974–75 an Amnesty International report estimated there to be over 25,000 political prisoners within Iran and its then Secretary-General asserted: 'The Shah of Iran retains his benevolent image despite the highest rate of death penalties in the world, no valid system of civilian courts and a history of torture which is beyond belief.'[25] The similarities between the two periods create an impression of the Islamic Republic as being quite as dogmatic and intolerant as any other one-party or authoritarian state.

Between 1979 and 1983 Khomeini and the Islamic Republican Party systematically destroyed all those who refused to support the government. Through the use of social and legal controls and the force of SAVAMA, it became possible to eliminate domestic opposition. The elections of 1980 and 1984 were strictly one-party affairs. The 1988 election was equally repressive in that individuals who had been permitted to stand were obliged to be screened and approved by local Islamic committees. With the demise of the Islamic Republican Party, one other party was recognized officially, the Nelzat Azadi (Liberation Movement of Iran) and allowed to participate in the 1988 elections on the grounds that it was an Islamic organization. Consequently, any consideration of Iranian political movements must focus on organizations operating in exile.

Exiled political groups

The Iranian opposition in Paris in the mid-1980s was formed into resistance groups which actively sought the overthrow of Khomeini. Bakhtiar, the former prime minister who was later, in 1991, to be assassinated, set up the National Movement of Iranian Resistance (NAMIR) to coordinate the activities of the liberal faction. According to reports in 1985 Bakhtiar maintained that he had a significant following in Iran because, unlike other oppositionist groups, he had warned the Iranian people about Khomeini before the repression began. He apparently felt uncompromised by accepting the premiership as he did so only on condition that the Shah agreed to restore free speech and press, terminate SAVAK and release political prisoners. NAMIR regularly transmitted short-wave radio broadcasts to Iran in order to expose the population to alternative views.[26] It is difficult to judge the efficacy of this operation at a time widely regarded to have been a period of terror. Just shortly after Khomeini died in November 1989, an official government statement proclaimed that the execution and torture of 'terrorists' was permitted under Islamic law.[27] Also by 1990 figures only 20 per cent of the population actually owned a radio set.[28]

Another organization, the National Council of Resistance (NCR) was established by Massoud Rajavi and Bani-Sadr to serve as an organizational centre for Islamic-oriented leftist opposition. Although in 1983 there was a rupture in relations between the two men over Rajavi's growing links with the Iraqi government which was conducting a war against Iran. Rajavi, in fact, was asked to leave France in 1986 and he moved to Iraq from where the following year he announced the formation of a National Liberation Army, 10,000–15,000 strong, as a military wing of the Mujahedin-Khalq. Dissident members of the Tudeh Party founded the Democratic Party of the Iranian People in Paris in 1988.

Perhaps, inevitably in parties existing in exile, all the groups believe the Islamic Republic has lost its credibility and popularity. Certainly, since the late 1980s there have been a series of mass demonstrations and food riots which have resulted in clashes with the Revolutionary Guard and a number of deaths. These activities suggested at the time that although the economy was disappointing in that levels of employment and efficiency were low, both of which clearly affected its popularity, the degree of repression was likely to inhibit political activity. Exiled political movements maintain that a new political consciousness directed against the government is developing amongst various sections of the population in Iran. This may be true, but there appears to be no coherent strategy on how to mobilize and direct such a movement. Another major shortcoming of the opposition rests in its internal divisions: the Liberal Nationalist NAMIR has little regard for the Islamic leftist-oriented NCR, and the possibilities of working together seem remote. It may be the case that the 'doctrine of Islamic resurgence has been on trial (in Iran) and may have been discredited by the excesses of the regime'.[29] Yet during the 1980s the Republic was essentially an absolutist state with no room for criticism from a population who, at times, displayed a disenchantment with the regime.

The glimmer of reform

On 28 July 1989, Hashemi Rafsanjani was elected Iran's new president and received 15.5 million of the 16.4 million votes cast.[30] However, a third of the electorate did not vote at all despite the fact that voting had been declared a religious duty by the government. Indeed rumours abounded that those who did not vote and accordingly did not have their identity cards appropriately stamped, would be considered 'counter revolutionaries'.

Rafsanjani's period of rule has marked a shift away from the Khomeini years, with promises of economic reform and so-called 'pragmatism'. Although political liberalization has not been on the agenda, human rights issues have elicited a response from the government. In September 1991 a human rights Conference was held in Tehran to which Western human rights activities and diplomats were invited. This occasion was widely seen as a sign that the Iranian government sought to end its international isolation and address some worrying domestic problems. Although the Human Rights Commission of the United Nations has been criticized by Iran for what is seen as its partiality and condemnation of the country's practices it was agreed at a later summit meeting of the Islamic Conference Organization, of which Iran is an influential member, that a special committee be established to study Islamic human rights and humanitarian issues.[31] For the first time in decades such topics were open to public debate within the country.

Diamond et al., in their studies of democratizing influences at play in various countries, maintain that 'the role of political leadership emerges in each case as an important factor'. Leadership is defined as 'the actions, values, choices and skills of a country's political elite and its one or few top government and party leaders'.[32] Rafsanjani is undoubtedly in a much stronger position than his predecessor. A national referendum held on election day, 28 July 1989, resulted in over 16 million votes being cast in favour of constitutional reforms which have enhanced the president's powers. The proposals drafted by the Council for the Study and Codification of the Amendments to the Constitution bestowed exclusive executive power on the president and abolished the position of prime minister. The president was empowered to appoint ministers, with the approval of the majlis and to take direct control of the country's economy. The majlis could, however, impeach the president, with a two-thirds majority vote.

Additionally, the president was appointed chairman of a new State Security Council which was created to formulate and coordinate Iran's security and defence policy and was formerly empowered to appoint a 20-member Expediency Council which would adjudicate on points of contention between the majlis and the Council of Constitutional Guardians. Rafsanjani saw himself as 'attempting to walk the middle way' and his 22-member cabinet, approved by the majlis, reflected his commitment to efficiency and included several Western-educated technocrats. These constitutional changes, however, have to be seen against the background of Iran's emergence from a damaging conflict. The war between Iran and Iraq which began when Iraq invaded Iran on 22 September 1980 and ended on 20 August 1988 has been interpreted as representing 'a test of the revolution, its capacity for commitment and sacrifice, as well as its ingenuity and self-reliance . . . It epitomised all the themes of suffering and martyrdom that the leadership seemed determined to cultivate.'[33] After Iran's acceptance of UN Security Council Ceasefire resolution 598 it was inevitable that some reforms would be introduced and there would be the internal factional struggle and jockeying for power usually associated with authoritarian regimes but a groundswell of opposition continued.

During 1991 a series of demonstrations again prompted by the increase in the price of staple foods led the government to defend its economic policy. But there have been further outbursts of public criticism, ranging from the protests and subsequent arrests of 300 women demonstrating against the Islamic dress code to charges of corruption, embezzlement and bribery against government officials.[34] There were also calls to Rafsanjani from the banned opposition group, the Iran Liberation Movement, to respect public freedoms and ensure that 'everyone has the right to criticise and protest and not simply those close to power'.[35] Again oppositionist radio reports in August 1991 interpreted the demonstrations as 'popular struggles' initially based on economic difficulties, namely the high cost and shortage of basic commodities, but ultimately leading to more overt political demands, that is, the overthrow of the Islamic Republic. The population were allegedly 'resolved to continue these demonstrations until the regime is toppled'.[36] Strikes and anti-government demonstrations did, indeed, continue and, interestingly, were always prompted by economic factors. In the government's eyes these outbursts have highlighted the importance of the economy to domestic stability, hence Rafsanjani's 'pragmatism', but they also clearly suggest the need for legitimate outlets for oppositionist opinion and this must imply some measure of political pluralism. However, whether such agitation and confrontation would actually lead to the overthrow of the regime is highly debatable. If change and reform is to come it will probably emerge from within the Islamic republic.

Post-Gulf War possibilities for reform

There can be no doubt that Iran's international profile improved radically following the 1991 Gulf War. Diplomatic links were advanced regionally and a *rapprochement* with the United States was achieved bringing economic benefits to the country. In March 1991 the United States agreed to permit American oil companies to purchase Iranian oil and Iran benefited from a World Bank loan of US$250 million, the first such transaction since 1978.

With the economy becoming increasingly important there may be some spin-offs in the political arena. Certainly, Iran's Permanent Representative to the United Nations, Dr Kamal Kharrazi, seemed to think so when he suggested that the Gulf War of 1991 raised the spectre of dictatorship which could only be combated by the promotion and strengthening of 'democratic institutions as well as checks and balances on government behaviour and procedures such as elections and parliaments'.[37] This statement was a far cry from Khomeini's last New Year address to the nation in which he reminded the population that priority should be given to continuing to crush the 'liberals', the agents of foreigners; their infiltrating elements and those who support them', in the pursuance of a universal Islamic state.[38] No mention at that time of the importance of establishing 'democratic institutions' or political accountability.

It may be possible that the amendments to the Electoral Act, ratified by the majlis in October 1991, ensuring that 'religious leaders, officials and all executive, judicial, military and law enforcement organs and revolutionary institutions must under no circumstances, indulge in propaganda in favour of or against any political group', will represent a significant move in the direction of institutional reform.[39] The major challenges confronting the republic would seem to be less of a religious dimension than those associated with the demands of a modern state: economic programmes of rationalization, unemployment, rising prices, strikes, foreign policy and an increasing awareness of domestic stability. Penetrate any state, of any political persuasion in the modern world, and those issues will be among its foremost concerns. The secular demands of the modernist state, political, economic and diplomatic may present an ultimatum to an Islamic republic.

Islamic democracy

Rafsanjani has spoken of the Islamic democratic alternative and pointed to the participatory nature of the Iranian political system. There have undoubtedly been regular elections in accordance with the conditions set down by the Islamic constitution, and 2000 candidates stood for 270 seats in the elections of April 1992. There were also occasions when recourse was made to the use of referenda. Clearly, then features identified as democratic form part of the political life of Iran. Political parties, of course, do not, but neither did they in states which often claimed to embrace 'socialist' democracy. If democratic centralism could not be compared directly with a liberal democratic multi-party competitive system of government, then, it might be argued, neither should an Iranian Islamic model. The Iranian system of democratic participation, therefore, must be judged on its own strengths and weaknesses, and perhaps more significantly, its capacity for change.

According to G. W. Choudhury, within an Islamic society, 'material progress or development must be achieved in the context of Islamic tradition, otherwise it is doomed to fail'.[40] Consequently, 'democratic order and the realisation of an ideal and fair society lies in the true spirit of Islam'.[41] But what does this precisely mean in the context of a functioning theocratic state? What exactly is the 'true spirit' of Islam? According to one analyst a distinction must be drawn between Islamic fundamentalism, as illustrated by the Shi'ite Iranian revolution of 1979 and Islamic liberalism as demonstrated in neighbourhood mosques and represented by an educated urban bourgeoisie.[42] Yet it must be acknowledged that if Islam is not a homogeneous religious movement in terms of political aspiration, the different spheres do, as Leonard Binder points out, 'draw on the same religious sources, often employ the same types of reasoning and concentrate on the same authoritative pronouncements'.[43] However, it is not unreasonable for religious movements or, indeed, political organizations to begin from a common base and then to subsequently diversify; inevitably, different denominations of Christian faith and various Marxist/Leninist/Trotskyist parties come to mind. The question here is whether a theocratic state conducts itself differently from any other state. Consequently, it is necessary to explore the parameters of such a state. As we have discussed, in the early days of the revolution, the Islamic Republic of Iran introduced policies and conducted itself in the manner of numerous post-revolutionary, authoritarian states, i.e., eliminated opposition, abolished political parties, firmly established control and so on. In such examples, it was often the case that if a war could be fought with an avowed enemy then so much the better for the regime's legitimacy and the nation's unity. But after the inevitable years of self-sacrifice and privation suffered by the population, and especially after the end of a period of conflict, the policies of those regimes shifted, sometimes to less ideological policies or, it might be argued, in the case of an Islamic state, to 'pragmatic' positions. When revolutionary states diluted ideological dogma they were often criticized for displaying 'revisionist' tendencies. Similarly, in the case of Rafsanjani's post-revolutionary Islamic republic, the adoption of 'pragmatic' policies might be regarded as 'irreligious' perhaps even, 'secular' proposals. In other words, a theocratic state can provide a mirror image of the usual model of a one-party state. The question which must be posed is whether it is possible for an Islamic state to reflect a multi-party, pluralistic mode of government?

Within this context, the Islamic notion of 'shura' can be employed. Elected representatives, within a national assembly, or majlis, deliberate, advise and engage in consultation and debate. The role played by the majlis holds the key to the extent to which democratization can occur. As we have seen Ayatollah Khomeini upon gaining power utilized elections and referenda. These policies could have represented either an Islamic recognition of the need for democratic structures or, alternatively, an abuse of those means of participation. The fundamental point of issue here is that democracy requires two essential conditions, adequate debate and accountability, irrespective of elections and referenda. Without those conditions a state will operate on an absolutist basis. One-party and authoritarian states are now condemned as reprehensible politically and dysfunctional in economic terms. Iran may find itself obliged to democratize simply because of the pressures of organizing a modern state, regardless of whether or not such policies are specified in the Qu'ran.

Conclusion

Of one central fact there would seem no question: political advancement in Iran suffered greatly from the deleterious impact of the Cold War. The polarized nature of the Shah's political stance and affinities and those of the Soviet-inclined Tudeh Party inevitably served to divide the nation's loyalties. The degree of repression utilized by the Shah, the security edifice constructed during those years, the creation of identikit parties and the general abuse of electoral processes debilitated political discourse and enabled Islamic leaders to become the alternative oppositionist force. Yet the political behaviour of Ayatollah Khomeini was as autocratic and repressive as any previous form of government. So what does this tell us about Iran's propensity for political reform?

It is, of course, not the first time that people have leapt at the chance of political change and then found themselves to be in pretty much the same position as before. Revolutions, by their very nature arousing such heightened political activity and sentiment, can augur a period of instability and repression. But the Islamic revolution seemed to promise much: a new reformist constitution, elections, referenda and above all a feeling that the country was at long last in control of its own political life and no longer possessed of a leader in thrall to the West. It was an attractive proposition and not unnaturally, it elicited considerable support. Also there existed a tradition within Iran of mullahs wresting powers away from authoritarian rulers and the events of 1979 could be viewed as no exception.

Quite what the Tudeh Party expected to gain from an Islamic republic is unclear. Participation in government always seemed unlikely, the most probable outcome being representation in the majlis had the first elections of the republic been bona fide. Whether the Tudeh Party then would have followed directives from the Soviet Union or followed its own counsel is open to debate but the important factor here is the degree of ideological polarization within the country which effectively pulled the nation in different directions: Westernization as perceived by the policies of the Shah and the White Revolution, negating a Persian inheritance or Marxist pro-Soviet which also represented an alien ideology. The paradox of the Cold War as it was played out in the Middle East is that the concept of opposing ideologies was a misleading one. In essence, both communism and liberal democracy stemmed from a European base and within that context could both be termed ideologies of 'Westernization'. A reassertion of an Islamic heritage in ethics and politics would be a way of displaying and distinguishing a nation's independence. As Arnold Toynbee defended the suitability of communism to countries in Asia and Africa in the 1950s on the grounds that it would give them the 'strength to stand up against the West',[44] in the 1970s Islam re-emerged as just such a force.

The fact that the Islamic republic under Ayatollah Khomeini conducted a level of domestic repression comparable to that of the Shah suggests that whichever complexion of regime there may be, secular or religious, a state which concedes no opposition will operate in the same manner. Bread riots will occur, demonstrations will take place, strikes will be called, deputations will be heard and the state will react with police action and imprisonment. If there are no legitimate channels for oppositionist opinion, other than through the party or the religious hierarchy, debate will be stifled and there will follow an inevitable recourse to repressive action. Rafsanjani, in common with the leadership of other Arab states in the region is considering democracy in terms of participation in elections and upholding the rights of a national assembly, which marks an improvement on the Shah's period, but the next vital step on the road to a fuller democracy is to permit opposition. The demonstrations in recent years clearly indicate the need for some degree of political pluralism. These actions are not, however, isolated incidents in one particular country but can be replicated in a number of Arab states. The moves represent a feature common to Iranian and Arab states in the post-Cold War years, that is, the indigenous tentative acknowledgement of the need for further democratization.

4 The dominant party state – Syria and Iraq

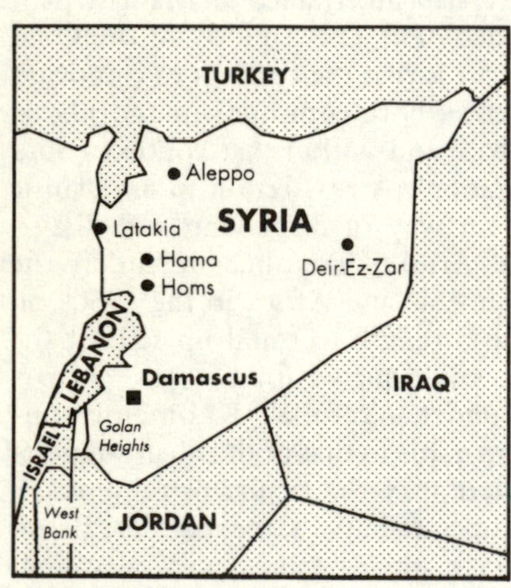

Samuel Huntington took the view that political parties could provide legitimacy and stability within a modernizing political system. They would act as mobilizing agents and accordingly, could assist in the construction of modern political institutions. The actions of government, therefore, could be legitimized inasmuch as they reflected the will of the party.[1] Ideologically, Ba'athism at its inception represented the classic 'means justifying ends' divide; a modernizing strategy which was profoundly attractive to post-colonial societies striving to forge their own identity and remove the yoke of dependency.

The Arab Socialist Ba'ath Party, the organization which paradoxically, still serves to link and separate Iraq and Syria was established in 1953, the result of a merger between the Arab Socialist Party led by Akram Hourani and the Arab Renaissance Party formed by Michel Aflaq and Salah Bitar. The Party's political stance emphasized social and economic reform; greater Arab unity through a form of pan-Arabism and the recognition of the relationship between Islam and Arabism. Essentially, it was a quasi-Marxist socialist party committed to a nationalized, redistributive economic system based on the principle of 'socialist nationalism', but which was to be strongly associated with an Arab identity. A Ba'ath Party document on Sectarianism, Regionalism and Tribalism, published in April 1966 stated: 'Arabism in its humanitarianism is the fundamental bond which binds people together and any other loyalty is a deviation because it is at the expense of that bond and is incompatible with the principles of nationalism which guarantee the progress of the Arab people.' Class antagonism would replace previous social animosities between Arab peoples based on regionalism, sectarianism or tribalism; elements which had rendered Arab society vulnerable to imperialism and exploitation. The party was to be built up in a 'firm, positive and homogeneous fashion'.[2] In fact, the process of purging the party of undesirable allegiances was seen to be an act of purification; a sign that the 'era of weakness and irresolution' was over. Strength was synonymous with the 'exercise of maximum levels of supervision, guidance and control in calling people to account'.[3]

One critic suggests that the party was never a mass movement for social change; instead of replacing social cleavages it merely grafted itself on to them. Others see the party as the creation of the 'urban intelligentsia' and not in any way the 'expression of clear social alignments or well-thought out integral domestic reform programmes'.[4] However, given the predominantly agrarian base of both Iraq and Syria in the 1950s, it would have been most unlikely for the party to have had industrial proletarian origins. The inevitability of factionalism in an ideologically based movement would always threaten and ultimately, in 1964, the breach between theoretical assumptions and practical application resulted in a party split and the development of two very different strands of Ba'athism, one in Syria, the other in Iraq.

This chapter will consider the different manifestations and orientations of the Ba'ath Party in those two countries and the extent to which they can be regarded as effective political entities, in terms of their contribution to reform and change. Again common features emerge in the case studies: external and indigenous activity, the impact of the Cold War, ideological division and competition, the question of pan-Arabism and the manner in which both countries handled those pressures.

Syria

The Ba'ath Party has dominated Syrian politics since 1963 and during the past thirty years has consolidated its authority. Before 1963 political institutions tended to be rather temporary affairs as the republican parliamentary structure collapsed in 1949, only three years after the country's independence from French colonial rule. The 1950s was characterized by a marked degree of political turbulence but one event was crucial: the formation of the United Arab Republic (UAR).

Pan-Arabism

The creation of the UAR and the union between Syria and Egypt put flesh on the bones of pan-Arabism and was widely supported by the Ba'ath party. It was not simply to be federalism, but fusion. The motivation, however, was not purely ideological; the union had a pragmatic dimension. It was as much for the survival of the Ba'ath Party as for any ideological reason, for the party felt menaced by the Syrian Communist Party and as the country refused to seek assistance from the West, Egypt was the obvious protector. The union proved, however, to be short-lived as Syria realized it meant being dominated by Egypt. The Ba'athists had in their enthusiasm for unity underestimated their own vulnerability. Nasser, who was now President of the UAR, was not enamoured of Ba'athist ideology and imposed a ban on all Syrian political parties together with seizure of the press. Political parties were replaced by the Cairo-directed National Union from which Ba'ath representatives were excluded. These measures kept the communist party in check but they hardly met the Ba'ath party's aspirations. The establishment of the UAR was a drastic move which lasted only three years and in September 1961 Nasser announced his intention to accept the separation of Syria from the association.

At first, Syria seemed unharmed by the experience but it had, in fact, created a groundswell of unrest between pro- and anti-Nasserists. The movement began to sever the Ba'ath Party, resulting in a military junta seizing control in 1963 only to be followed by a damaging series of coups d'état as the country lurched between the two wings of the party. The ideological schism centred on how to restructure Syrian society. One element favoured a one-party state, the creation of agricultural cooperatives, workers' management, and the reallocation of land to the peasantry; policies which were regarded as minimal socialist measures designed to restructure society. The alternative view rejected those policies as too radical, on the grounds that they would disrupt the domestic political scene. Aflaq and Bitar the founding members of the party, sympathized with the latter view and in a clash between the two groups in 1964, the two men were accused of betraying the basic principles of the party and they fled the country. Party division was fuelled when, because the pan-Arab movement had been found wanting, Syria began to shift towards the Soviet Union who provided military aid along with economic and technical assistance. To some Ba'athists this dependency was tantamount to neo-colonialism and further upheaval followed when Syria suffered the loss of the Golan Heights in the Six Day War with Israel in June 1967.

There was scarcely any doubt that the events of the 1960s had a devastating effect on Syria's political system. The country had no functioning constitution, only a series of temporary proposals; there had been no parliament of any description since 1966 and rapid changes of leadership had created an environment which bordered on political disintegration. It was only a matter of time before a leader, of one form or another, emerged to take charge of the country; and that is precisely where Assad came in.

Constitutional/parliamentary reform

Lt General Hafiz al-Assad became Prime Minister and Party General Secretary as the result of yet another coup d'état in November 1970. Thereafter, a new Regional Command was formed and the party was duly purged of its former leaders. By March 1971 Assad was elected President for a seven-year term, and he has remained in power for over twenty years. Assad, however, introduced a series of political changes. A new and permanent constitution was endorsed by the electorate in a national referendum on 12 March 1973. Under the 157-article constitution which defines Syria as a 'socialist popular democracy' with a 'pre-planned socialist economy' President Assad appoints vice-presidents and the executive body, the Council of Ministers. The legislature, the 195-member People's Assembly, is elected for a four-year term on a constituency basis. There is universal adult suffrage and voting is compulsory.

However, one political feature which differentiates Syria from other states and is also one of Assad's strengths is the composition of the National Progressive Front (NPF). The Front was formed in 1972 by a national charter and comprises five parties: the Arab Socialist Party; the Arab Socialist Unionist Party, both off-shoot socialist parties; the Syrian Arab Socialist Union Party, a pan-Arab, Nasserite organization, the Communist Party of Syria and, of course, the Ba'ath Party. Although the component parts of the Front appear to be variants on a theme in that they are all left of centre, Independents may stand in elections. As such, the regime has broadened its political base at the same time as providing a semblance of opposition. In the elections for the new People's Council in 1973, 140 of the then 186 available seats were won by the Progressive Front, whilst the remainder were won by Independents.[5] This multi-party system in which parties operate within a form of popular front is not unknown in liberal democracies and at its best can provide a functioning coalition. It might also lend itself to a consociational model of political interaction. But there exists one central factor in the Syrian system: there is no parity between the parties. According to Article 7 of the constitution the Ba'ath Party is 'the leading party of the society and state' which essentially places it in a pre-eminent position and underpins its power and authority. Nevertheless, it must be acknowledged that the electorate is provided with some degree of choice at election time and the distribution of cabinet posts can embrace different shades of opinion. For example, in 1976 the NPF won 159 of the increased figure of 195 seats in the People's Assembly and formed a coalition with 36 cabinet posts only half of which were Ba'athists. The other members included two Communists, two Arab Socialist Union, three Unionist Socialist Movement, two Arab Socialist Party and nine Independents.[6] Yet this political structure has failed to prevent opposition to the regime.

Islamic opposition to regime

One of the most serious challenges to Ba'athist political dominance has come from Sunni Islamic fundamentalism. In February 1982 an uprising lasting three weeks took place in Hama. It was eventually suppressed by Assad's forces with considerable loss of life, and although it was primarily led by the Islamic group, the Muslim Brotherhood other oppositionist elements participated. During that period an organization called the National Alliance of the Syrian People was formed which consisted of 19 factions drawn from disaffected Ba'athists, Nasserists, Christians and members of the Muslim Brotherhood. Interestingly, this movement, under another name, the National Alliance for Liberation of Syria, emerged again in 1989. Muhammad Umar Burhan, a member of its General Secretariat, announced in Geneva that 'Syrian opposition parties and people's organisations had organised meetings and agreed to establish a broad-based national front, the major objective of which is the institution of a democratic regime which would undermine the power of President Assad'.[7] Reports from Paris in 1990 referred to the formation of an 'all-Syrian opposition movement called the Patriotic Front for National Salvation, which apparently comprised political and religious organizations and parties, including the Muslim Brotherhood who agreed to cooperate with nationalist and non-religious groups. This particular Patriotic Front called for the overthrow of President Assad, 'by armed struggle if the people wish' and for the establishment of a multi-party parliamentary system.[8] The revealing aspect of this development was the fact that the Front was to be financed by Iraq and based in Baghdad. It is, of course, difficult to assess whether its ambitions were genuine or if it was being used by Syria's arch-enemy and co-Ba'athist state, for spurious purposes. There has been no mention of the organization since the 1991 Gulf War.

However, one should not underestimate the opposition of the Muslim Brotherhood to what is regarded as: 'a secularist, anti-Islamic, sectarian Alawi regime'.[9] The domination of the majority Sunni population by Assad's own Alawi community who represent 10 per cent of a population of 12 million, has remained a focus of tension. The Muslim Alawites are, in fact, an unorthodox Shi'ite sect. As Michael Hudson states: 'While the Alawites do not exhibit marked linguistic or ethnic differences from other Syrians, they are regarded by the majority as different, secretive, and to some extent suspect.'[10] However, although the Syrian constitution proclaims Islam to be the religion of the Head of State, it does not encompass Islam as the religion of the state itself. In a sense, Islam of the Sunni variety presents a challenge not only to President Assad but also to the Ba'ath Party, especially as between 70–75 per cent of the population are Sunni Muslim.[11]

The minority status of the regime is inescapable and one of Assad's strengths is his control of the army. It is maintained that of the military members of the Syrian Regional Commands since 1975 Assad has relied to an 'important extent on officers from his own family, tribe or village neighbourhood'.[12] This policy has allegedly reduced factionalism within the military and enhanced discipline and political stability within the regime.[13] However, it must not be forgotten that an abortive coup attempt in 1976 against Assad's regime apparently resulted from resentment against Alawi supremacy. Alawi dominance also undermines the regime on other fronts, namely through charges of corruption and political unaccountability.

Opposition to corruption

At the end of the 1970s there was widespread popular discontent with the government's economic policy and more precisely the level of corruption which allegedly ran through government bureaucracy and the public sector. Assad responded by introducing an anti-corruption campaign in the form of a Committee for Investigation of Illegal Profits which was established to 'investigate crimes of bribery, imposition of influence, embezzlement, exploitation of office and illegal profits'.[14] It was discovered that those guilty of engaging in corrupt practices were, in fact, highly placed military officers, predominantly Alawi, who were stalwarts of Assad's regime. Clearly, to take action against these officers would have undermined Assad's position. Consequently, the anti-corruption campaign failed at that time but the issue was to reappear. Between 1980 and 1985, there were two anti-corruption purges and some public officials were hanged but the issue remained a contentious one.[15] The corruption was judged to stem from what many believe over the past decade to be the party's mishandling of the economy, more particularly, state interference. The party congress in 1985 certainly seemed responsive to criticism and placed the question of reform on its agenda. Indeed, according to reports at the time Assad took the proceedings so seriously that he did not allow the congress to do its work in committees, as was customary. Instead, he attended every one of the plenary sessions for 14 days, the length of the congress.

It might be considered to be a mark of Assad's political astuteness to encourage openness and debate in what has been termed a 'people's party', although such levels of discussion are not generally regarded as the norm. But the permission granted to delegates to speak freely of the extent of corruption in public affairs raised problems for Assad because of the familial nature of his regime. His brother, Rifaat, head of the Defence Brigade, had come into prominence at the end of 1983 when Assad suffered a period of illness. For a few months there was the beginning of a power struggle which threatened open conflict until Assad sent his brother to Moscow and re-asserted his authority. Rifaat returned six months later but his return aroused suspicions. In short, there were two central questions confronting the party congress in 1985: first, the appalling problem of corruption with which Rifaat had been associated and second, the problem of succession and the role of the President's brother. The congress, despite being granted a carte blanche on discussion found itself to be in something of a dilemma. Rifaat as controller of national security and a third-ranking vice-president of the country, was still very much in the running as possible successor to Assad. There was clearly unlikely to be an effective anti-corruption campaign as long as Rifaat remained in a senior party and state position. These kinds of problems, however, are characteristic of a disproportionate distribution of power and authority and a narrow elite base. They are not necessarily a feature of a dominant party state which operates a meritocratic system, although it is not unknown for favoured party members to retain their positions; but the Syrian republic combined the frailties of the authoritarian structure with the obvious, anachronistic tendencies of filial and tribal loyalties. Instead of the Ba'ath Party 'modernizing' the country's political system it appeared to attach itself to existing methods of political exchange.

Political reforms

In 1990 reports emerged that in light of the changes in Eastern Europe the government was planning a series of initiatives to liberalize both economic and political practices. Syria, of course, was regarded in the West as a satellite state of the Soviet Union. Reports often asserted that the secret of Assad's success in controlling domestic opposition depended on a combination of 'a massive if sometimes divided repressive apparatus and friendship with the Soviet Union'.[16] The political reform and disintegration of the Soviet empire was the catalyst for the introduction of liberalizing policies in Syria, in much the same way as they have occasioned changes in other Third World countries.

Immediately, in 1990 the Council of Ministers announced its intention to abolish martial law regulations which had been originally introduced during the UAR period, 1958–61. A law setting up special courts to investigate criminal cases involving government employees was issued by Assad, which was widely regarded to be an attempt to strengthen the government's anti-corruption campaign.[17] The People's Assembly was expanded from 195 to 250 seats and the elections held in May 1990 resulted in a larger allocation of seats to independent candidates. Although the Ba'ath Party retained its dominant position its proportion of seats fell from 66 per cent in 1986 to 54 per cent in 1990 (see Table 4.1). Over 9700 candidates competed in the elections and a turnout of just over 60 per cent was officially recorded. The number of women in the Assembly increased by 18 to 21. Obviously, it is not straightforward to assess the undercurrents of an election in a country as closed as Syria, or indeed, to examine the extent of opposition

Table 4.1 Seats gained in the general elections to the People's Assembly

	22/23 May 1990	*10/11 February 1986*
Ba'th Party	134	129
Other National Progressive Front Parties	32	31
Independent	84	35
Total	250	195

Source: *Keesings Records of World Events*, May 1990, Vol. 36, No. 5.

to the regime. A 60 per cent turnout in a general election where voting is compulsory may suggest apathy, disenchantment, passive opposition or lax administration.

However, the results have been overshadowed by the impact of the 1991 Gulf War. Syria reaped great political and economic benefits from the Gulf crisis. President Assad's decision to support the United States'-led anti-Iraq alliance following Iraq's invasion of Kuwait has contributed to an international reappraisal of the country and its consequent rehabilitation. The Treaty of Brotherhood and Cooperation signed with Lebanon in the summer of 1991 links the two countries at a structural political level and has further enhanced Syria's authority.[18] According to the publication, 'Al-Ba'ath', it was very natural for Syria and Lebanon to form such a close association as both countries' ties and roots 'go deep in history: the one blood and the common hopes, aspirations, culture, traditions and customs'.[19] Whatever the similarities and affinities between the two nations, and it must be remembered that elements within Syria have had designs on Lebanon for years, one aspect is quite clear: there has never been a commonality between the two countries' political systems, despite their mutual French colonial heritage. The 'Socialist Popular Democracy' of Syria does not compare with Lebanon's confessional form of democratic government.

Whether Syria's new commitment to political and economic pluralism will liberalize Syrian society is unclear. However, at a meeting of the Regional Command of the Ba'ath Party in November 1991 an agreement was made unanimously to recommend the nomination of Hafiz al-Assad for a 'new constitutional term' as President and was duly presented to the People's Assembly. To observers of Syrian politics there was nothing remarkable about the decision. The procedure was quite commonplace; Assad's presidency had been renewed since 1971. Nevertheless, included in the recommendation was a statement containing a number of aims, principles and objectives regarding the political and economic direction the country should follow. The first priority was that 'the democratic march of the country be bolstered by the enhanced role to be played by democratic institutions elected by the people; second, political pluralism, popular organizations and professional associations would all be stressed; third, the country would be committed to economic prosperity and should secure the widest possible participation by citizens in economic development within the framework of economic pluralism.[20]

These statements laid down a clear set of objectives for a country which until very recently had been referred to as 'a strict police state without the slightest indication of political liberalisation', and seem to indicate a shift in the political direction of the Ba'ath Party.[21] Whether moves towards greater pluralism would automatically undermine the Party's position in a state which already permits the existence of other political parties is debatable. Any move which diminished the role of the party would, of course, require an amendment to the constitution. Yet until the end of the Cold War it would have been difficult to imagine such a debate even taking place.

Conclusion

Huntington's views on the legitimizing and stabilizing effects produced by political parties appears to have been borne out by the experience of the Ba'ath Party in Syria especially under the leadership of President Assad. According to one analyst the 'unity principle gave the party a degree of legitimacy that helped compensate for its small size and lack of popularity . . . the party structure provided the security and durability for the Ba'ath to survive its attackers and outlast its competitors'.[22] Ba'athism, defined in Syria as 'socialist nationalism' has undoubtedly endured the decades in a way which the Nasser movement and other groups and organizations have not. So why is this the case? Does the answer rest in the party or in the country?

The party had, at its inception, an Arab dimension but then so did numerous other socialist and nationalist organizations. It is possible to remember Nasser's commitment to the 'Arab road to socialism' and the role Egypt should play in pan-Arabism. Equally, if Syrians are to share the same 'primordial' characteristics of their 'brothers' in Lebanon or, indeed, their foes in Iraq, in other words if Arabness and consequently, pan-Arabism is to have any real meaning, why should Ba'athism succeed in certain countries and not others. The clue to finding the answer resides in the impact of the Cold War on a country such as Syria. Syria was largely protected by the Soviet Union and consequently reviled by the West. Its political structures and orientation meshed with the political disposition of the then USSR, in a way similar to several Third World countries who followed the Soviet model of development. The Syrian Communist Party formed part of the National Front, a fully legitimate participant in an important coalition in stark contrast to its proscribed status in a number of neighbouring states. If anything the Cold War worked to Syria's advantage: there were no accusations of Assad being a 'puppet' of the Soviet Union and the absence of oil resources minimized Western interest and contention, in contrast to the Iraqi experience. Syria was a sphere of interest in the super-power struggle for containment in the Middle East, avowedly pro-Soviet, anti-American and most importantly, hardline anti-Israeli. In a sense, Syria's association with the Soviet Union helped to stabilize the country and allowed the party to consolidate its authority.

So what are the prospects for democratization? Whether the violent overthrow of the Assad regime would necessarily herald democratic, representative, parliamentary government is certainly open to debate. In any case, the likelihood of the Ba'ath government being overthrown by either a military coup or an Islamic uprising now seems remote. Clearly, then, attention must focus on the possibilities for reform emanating from the party itself.

The party has been important, not necessarily as a vehicle for articulating demands but as an organization adept at coalescing political debate within its formal structures, and this has been its greatest strength. The formation of the National Front could, in fact, be seen as an enlightened example of consensual politics in a region not especially noted for its toleration but, of course, the negative aspect is the level of inequality between the party and the other political organizations and the uneven dispensation of power and authority. Whether the party possessed a modernizing political function is a debatable point, but there has been societal differentiation at the economic level which has contributed to the creation of professional associations. Political choice at electoral level has widened but the familial, tribal, minority inheritance of the elite remains. Until this feature changes the party will be vulnerable to criticism and may, on the demise of President Assad, be regarded as a temporary feature of twentieth-century politics. As Edmund Burke stated, a state lacking means of change is without the means of its conservation. And that is precisely the unknown quantity regarding Syria now: the extent to which reform can come from within. It is one thing for a nation to announce a change of policy because a protector state has altered its political course, but quite another for indigenous reform to be completely implemented. Such a move would imply the diminution of the power of Assad and his coterie within the party, and perhaps, more significantly, the absolute decline of the party as a whole.

Of course, it is in the nature of political life for parties to change into all manner of hybrid forms, but the chief factor in a party's continued existence is its capacity to change at times of necessity. If democracy, perhaps of a consociational form, is to flourish in Syria, and the possibilities do exist, particularly as such a system of government has now returned to Lebanon, the Ba'ath Party will need to reconsider certain fundamental principles, at risk in the short term to its own power but vital in the long term to its longevity.

Iraq

There is considerable difference in the way in which the Ba'ath Party operates in Syria and Iraq, and the degree to which other parties are tolerated or simply banned. M. and P. Sluglett, in their study of Iraq, point out that the party has made a 'major contribution' to 'regime stability' but as to whether this fact can be judged to be a 'positive or negative achievement must be open to question'.[23] Iraq has, of course, experienced a variety of internal and external pressures which have wrought an impact on its political structures, and led to a belief that strong central government and political leadership is, perhaps, inevitable. These views stem from the country's alleged lack of coherence resulting from the artificial nature of its creation, courtesy of the British and the ethnic and religious divisions which have plagued the nation. The country is, of course, essentially divided into component sections: Kurdish north, Iraqi centre and Shi'ite south and has always suffered from the threat of division or secession, unlike neighbouring Syria who historically sought to re-extend its boundaries and coveted Lebanon. Also Iraq had substantial oil wealth and consequently was a nation of economic importance in the context of the Cold War. The Iran–Iraq war, a conflict which lasted eight years, placed its political structures under severe strain, with the suspected potential uprising of the Shi'ites in sympathy with Iran coupled with Kurdish rebellion, and raised to a new height the spectre of domestic opposition. Yet the prospect of pan-Arabism, inherent in Ba'athist tradition, is a torch still burning, this time with Iraq at the head. When Saddam Hussein consolidated his grip on power in 1980 he announced: 'The glory of Arabs stems from the glory of Iraq. Throughout history whenever Iraq became mighty and flourished, so did the "Arab Nation". This is why we are striving to make Iraq mighty, formidable, able and developed.'[24] The Ba'ath Party in Iraq, then, still represents certain identifiable notions characteristic of its original ideology and in that way continues to maintain a level of legitimacy.

Parliament/constitution

Whilst Iraq was still under British mandatory influence an 'Organic Law' was established in 1924 which remained Iraq's constitution until 1958. The 'Law' established a bi-cameral parliamentary system in which the monarch, King Faisal, retained the power to appoint and dismiss ministers. A formal political life 'operated in an almost entirely artificial atmosphere and occupied itself very little with the major political and economic concerns of the population'.[25] By the early 1950s, the government was seen to be corrupt and self-interested and far too closely identified with the United States and Britain. By early 1957 the three main opposition parties, banned in 1954, the National Democratic Party (NDP), the Iraqi Communist Party (ICP) and the Ba'ath Party, had formed the National Unity Front. The Front was a very loose alliance mainly because its component parties were so diverse. The NDP, small in number, was essentially, a 'liberal' party of the Iraqi bourgeoisie: its aim was a kind of reformist revolution, rather more on the lines of the French Revolution than the Russian model of 1917. The ICP was, of course, strongly linked with the former Soviet Union and although its supporters saw it as a party of social justice and economic amelioration, its objectives were honed on the Soviet experience. Its central concern was to mobilize and unify all political forces opposed to the regime and it attracted considerable support. The Ba'ath Party at that time was small and factionalized.

The parties were able to sustain the Front by espousing anti-government sentiments and favouring social and land reform. Nevertheless, they did not participate in the revolutionary military coup d'état which took place in 1958 against what was seen as a reactionary and unrepresentative government. The coup, headed by Brigadier Abd al-Karim Qasim, resulted in the execution of King Faisal and members of the royal family. Qasim became Prime Minister and effective President of the newly proclaimed people's republic. According to public announcements, the new regime was to emanate from the people and would work to uphold complete Iraqi unity.[26] However, when the new cabinet was announced neither the Iraqi Communist Party nor the Kurdish Democratic Party were invited to participate. Qasim's social and political policies were welcomed by a wide-spectrum of Iraqi society in that, in many respects they met former demands: a programme of land reform; rent reductions; trade union recognition; food subsidies; evacuation of British bases; closer alliances with socialist countries and a greater share of oil royalties, but it was not long before the new President announced that elections would be delayed. The main contradiction in Iraq immediately after the coup centred on the political direction the regime would take. In short, would it travel down the totalitarian road whilst making promises of abundance to the population or would it choose a more democratic path? In reality, Iraq was not operating in a political vacuum; the coup had obviously attracted the attention of the West who feared an increased role for the communists. According to the director of the CIA, the situation in Iraq was 'the most dangerous in the world today' and he was convinced the communists were close to a 'complete takeover'.[27] This statement was not simply Cold War rhetoric but a declaration of the CIA's extreme concern regarding the United States' oil interests in the Middle East. It was quite possible that if elections were to take place the Communist Party could win substantially and reorient the country.

The Cold War

The Qasim government fell in 1963, the victim of another coup, this time, however, the circumstances had changed. The coup was orchestrated by the Ba'ath Party with the assistance of the CIA who had allegedly provided the Ba'athists with the 'names and addresses of communist leaders'. As a result 'five thousand communists and pro-Qasim sympathisers were killed in the first three days of the coup as Ba'athist gangs carried out house-to-house searches and on-the-spot executions'.[28] Whatever the precise role of the CIA there can be little doubt that the 1963 coup, carried out by Ba'athist-led forces, by then fervently opposed to communism, approximated Western interests. It was a brutal coup which the Ba'ath Party acknowledged. The Political Report of the Eighth Regional Congress of the Party held in Baghdad in January 1974 openly stated: 'In the revolution of February 1963 blood was shed freely', and any future seizures of power would have to be taken 'without such bloodletting [which] would spoil the image and divert the course of the revolution, reviving memories of the bloody events of 1963'.[29] Certainly, the report issued by the British Committee for the Defence of Human Rights in Iraq, in 1964, compared the coup with the actions of 'Hitlerite shock troops' prepared to use violence gratuitously, and Hanna Batatu's descriptions of the torture chambers of Qasr al-Nihayah in Baghdad, a palace which had become a centre for detention and interrogation, make grim and sobering reading.[30]

It is still difficult to judge quite how the Qasim government would have fared. It had embarked on an agrarian reform programme and had passed the so-called Law 80 in October 1961 which attempted to limit the concessionary rights of the Iraq Petroleum Company in favour of the government. With 53 per cent of the Iraqi labour force employed in agriculture in 1960 these measures clearly had a popular dimension.[31] Yet Qasim had succeeded in isolating himself from political groupings and had placed himself in virtual political seclusion. Also there were the tremendous problems of the Kurdish population and their quest for autonomous status. The Kurds, in pursuit of autonomy, had throughout 1962 been able to consolidate their hold over much of northern Iraq and although there were moves to recognize Kurdish claims in a new Constitution, there was no readiness on the part of the Kurds to cease opposition to the government until their claims were met. The Kurds formed only 18 per cent of the population but their political aspirations, resulting from statelessness, were finely tuned and would continue to be so, especially when forged with an ideological imperative. There can be little doubt that the revolution of 1958 revealed a 'Pandora's box' within Iraq: a country riven with ideological currents and ethnic division only to be exacerbated by oil resources and super power Cold War rivalry.

Ideological divisions

As was the case in Syria, the years between 1963 and 1968 were characterized by political uncertainty and incoherence: 'All hope of the establishment of any form of democratic political life based on representative institutions had been crushed and a system emerged which had no other source of legitimacy except that conferred by military force.'[32] In common with other developing nations military coup followed military coup as factions sometimes within the Ba'ath Party, sometimes not, struggled for power. The Ba'ath Party returned to power in July 1968 with the stated goals of 'liberation, democracy, socialism and Arab unity'.[33] Others were to perceive its true aims as the defeat of any attempts at democratic development.[34] Whatever the rhetoric of the period, this government was quickly replaced by yet another coup orchestrated by a group of disaffected army officers and 'rightist' elements within the party. Major General Ahmad Hasan al-Bakr was proclaimed President and there followed a period of 'consolidation of the revolutionary government' under the party's leadership, although with very little indication of precisely which policies would be followed.[35]

One especially interesting feature of the ideological division within the country was the relationship between the Iraqi Communist Party and the Ba'ath Party. The 1968 government made conciliatory overtures to the ICP in an attempt to absorb opposition. The communists were reportedly amazed to be offered three ministerial portfolios from a party which only five years previously had organized a reign of terror against them.[36] The ICP regarded the Ba'ath Party as 'a petite bourgeois nationalist party' which was anti-imperialist but had dictatorial and anti-democratic tendencies. There was nothing terribly surprising about this assessment but the communists decided upon a strategy: a list of basic demands would be presented to the government, i.e. the elimination of terror and the restoration of democratic constitutional life; a democratic solution of the Kurdish problem, on the basis of autonomy; securing people's economic and social rights; eliminating spy networks and strengthening the struggle against imperialism and Zionism.[37] However, the demands were adopted as part of the Ba'ath Party's avowed objectives which put the ICP in a difficult position, it could scarcely fully oppose a government which had embraced its demands. By the ICP's Second National Congress in 1970 the party was facing a dilemma but had placed itself firmly on the fence:

> We will continue on the same basis of opposition and criticism of whatever is negative and wrong, opposing the anti-democratic policy of the government and its suppression of all parties, of its narrow nationalism and its violation of human rights . . . But at the same time we shall support and back any progressive measure or any firm stand against colonialism, Zionism, feudalism and reaction.[38]

The Ba'ath Party's provisional constitution issued in 1968 had proclaimed the Iraqi Republic to be a 'popular democratic and sovereign state' with Islam as its religion. The democratic rights of the population were outlined:

> The state will protect liberty of religion, freedom of speech and opinion. Public meetings are permitted under law. All discrimination based on race, religion or language is forbidden. There shall be freedom of the press, and the right to form societies and trade unions in conformity with the law, is guaranteed.[39]

On paper it all looked very encouraging and in 1973, the two parties signed the National Action Charter which formed the National Patriotic Front, stipulating that relations between the parties would be 'based on mutual respect for the independence of each other, ideologically, politically and organisationally'.[40] Some commentators refer to the ICP's willingness to join the Front as an act of suicide.[41] It certainly seemed a case of 'supping with the devil'. Yet paradoxically, the Ba'ath Party viewed the communists with suspicion and fear. The Central Report of the 9th Regional Congress of the Ba'ath Party, published in 1982, provides an interesting account of the alliance period. Referring to its association with the ICP, the report stated:

> It was not possible within the framework of the unstable relationship with the ICP leadership to set up democratic institutions . . . Would it have been correct, frankly speaking to provide a new platform from which the ICP leadership could use the cover of the Front to defame the Party and the revolution and implement foreign strategies? The delay in setting up the National Assembly is thus partly due to this reason.[42]

Accepting there may have been a measure of *post hoc* rationalization in the Ba'ath Party's defence of its undemocratic structures and lack of a legislative body, the Report believed the ambitions of the ICP encompassed the possibilities of Iraq becoming a satellite state of the Soviet Union.

Other commentators adopt a more exacting view of the cooperation between the communists and Ba'athists, maintaining that it was one of vacillation between 'need and convenience'. After the conclusion of the Iraqi-Soviet Treaty in 1972, the Ba'ath regime was apparently encouraged by the Soviet Union to initiate 'formal co-operation with the Communist Party'.[43] Whilst the government felt vulnerable both in its foreign relations and economic base it sought an alliance with the ICP. However, when the economy improved following the massive oil price rises in 1973/74 which saw oil revenues soar from US$575 million in 1972 to US$5700 million in 1974 and the signing of the Algiers Agreement on 15 June 1975 which delineated Iraq's position in the Shatt al-Arab waterway dispute with Iran as well as preventing Iranian support to the Kurdish community, the alliance became less necessary to the government.[44]

There was undoubtedly a discernible shift in the attitude of the regime to the communists between 1976 and 1979. The association between the two parties was probably the result of a synthesis of motivations, and a distinct element of *realpolitik*. Whilst the reactions of the Communist Party may appear masochistic in its apparent desire for self-inflicted injury, it must be remembered that the strategy of indigenous communist parties was notoriously ill-judged in a number of Middle Eastern countries during that period. Unlike their counterparts in Syria, the Iraqi communists paid a high price for their participation. The Ba'ath party, in its newspaper 'al-Thawrah' announced that 'the revolutionary punishment of execution' would be passed against any member of a political party who 'tried to penetrate the armed forces'.[45] There was unlikely to be a more efficient way of keeping the lid on political activity especially as members of the ICP found themselves once again the victims of arrest and imprisonment. Iraq had found a new confidence as a result of its increased oil wealth, not only in its domestic political repression but also externally, as one analyst put it: 'Baghdad remained a free agent, shooting local communists and making overtures to the west from time to time'.[46] By late July 1979 the Central Committee of the ICP declared the party's open opposition to the Ba'ath regime under the slogan: 'For a Democratic Patriotic Front to End the Dictatorship and Establish a Democratic System of government in Iraq' which, rather longwindedly, marked the end of the alliance. It is perhaps inevitable that newly found oil wealth would liberate Iraq from the necessity to curry favour with the communists or indeed the USSR, a freedom which, of course, Syria did not share. Communist parties of that era followed the directive of the Soviet Union and despite their calls for democracy, were not above instituting political control themselves through the organ of the one-party state. If the Ba'ath Party could be manipulated by whomever, equally the ICP could reflect Soviet ambitions in the area be they policies of aggrandizement, containment or destabilization.

Ethnic factors

The plight of the Kurdish peoples divided by the imperialist powers in 1920 between Iraq, Iran and Turkey and denied a separate state created a particular manifestation of primordial loyalties as help and assistance was provided to the community across borders. The Ba'ath Party hoped that the conflict between the Kurds and the Iraqi government would end when Iran agreed not to provide assistance to the community as part of the Algiers Agreement of 1975. As a consequence, the Kurdish peoples were transferred to other areas and under these circumstances their leaders were obliged to reorganize, eventually into two rival factions: the Kurdish Democratic Party (KDP) led by Mas'ud Barzani and the Patriotic Union of Kurdistan (PUK) led by Jalal Talabani. Although, the PUK organization claimed to be basing its policies on a 'Marxist Leninist ideology', its relations with the ICP were strained. The communists regarded PUK as a 'pseudo-Marxist faction' and despite difficulty in discerning precisely what that term of abuse meant, it clearly did serve to further divide and lessen the potency of opposition.

Saddam Hussein became President of Iraq in July 1979, the result of yet another coup d'état and instituted a purge among the top echelon of the Ba'ath Party. The former president was executed along with one-third of the members of the Revolutionary Command Council. The early policies of the Hussein regime shifted against the USSR allegedly on account of its invasion of Afghanistan and in favour of some form of *rapprochement* with the West. Interestingly, legislation, published in December 1979, provided the ground plan for the first elections to be held in the country for 22 years. It specified there should be a National Assembly of not less than 250 members, elected by free and direct suffrage every four years and that members of the ruling Revolutionary Command Council (RCC) should be members of the Assembly. Also in the three Kurdish areas of Arbil,

Dihok, and Sulaymaniyah, 50 members should be elected to the Kurdish Legislative Council under the same conditions, for three-year terms. These bills were presented for popular debate and were ratified by the RCC in March 1980. The National Assembly would, alongside the RCC, perform legislative duties and 'supervise the state's institutions; propose and enact laws in accordance with the constitution; ratify the state budget as well as international treaties and agreements; debate the state's internal and foreign policy; summon any cabinet member for clarification or questioning and propose the relieving of any cabinet member of his post.'[47]

Elections to the National Assembly were held in June 1980 with 840 candidates contesting 250 seats. Although candidates did not identify themselves with political parties, the control of the Assembly was exercised by adherents of the Ba'ath Party. At first sight and given their obvious limitations, these moves did seem to represent a slight move in a democratic direction but the situation was not so clear cut. On 22 September 1980 Iraqi forces advanced into Iran and less than two months later, on 12 November, an alliance of opposition groups under the umbrella title: the Democratic Patriotic and National Front (DPNF) was formed in Syria. The DPNF included the Iraqi Communist Party; the Arab Socialist Movement, the Socialist Party, and the pro-Syrian faction of the Ba'ath Party. The Front supported the Patriotic Union of Kurdistan (PUK) and advocated 'the overthrow of the dictatorial regime and the setting up of a patriotic coalition government which will achieve democracy for Iraq and autonomy for Iraqi Kurdistan'.[48] The DPNF, however, was to be beleaguered by factionalism and by 1983 began to disintegrate.

The eight-year war between Iran and Iraq raised problems for ethnic groups who were suspected of disloyalty. It was believed at the time that a secret alliance of Iraqi Shi'as and Kurds backed by Iran's revolutionary armies, would present a real internal danger to Saddam Hussein, given that half of Baghdad's population of 2.5 million were Shi'a. The potential threat to the regime resulted in the government's manipulation of possible opposition from Shi'a groups and to the attempted Islamization of the Ba'ath Party. By declaring the Iranian revolution to be a Persian rather than an Arab Islamic uprising, Saddam Hussein managed to play the non-Arab, second-class Muslim, racial card and present the party as a representation of Islam.[49] Not only did the party make public declarations of deference to Islam but its president announced that the party's 'inspiration derived from Islam'.[50] The Ba'ath Party, of course, was not above assuming the features of other organizations; only twenty years previously it had eagerly adopted the policies of the Communist Party in an attempt to attract support within the country. It adopted chameleon-like tactics if the occasion demanded or if basic survival dictated such.

Whilst espousing Islamist sentiments, the RCC expelled 'thousands of people, reportedly tens of thousands of Shi'ites under the pretext of their alleged 'Iranian origin'.[51] Later, the Islamic Da'wa organization was banned, membership of which was made punishable by death and the Shi'a leader

Sayyid Muhammad Baquir al-Sadr was executed. Reports in 1985 suggested that the Iraqi regime was strong and oppositionist forces had failed to crystallize into an actual threat. The Shi'ite community as a whole remained 'very passive' not because they were necessarily persuaded by the Islamic utterings emanating from the RCC but more probably because the government was making 'concerted efforts' to improve social and economic conditions in the south.[52] The attraction of Islam has been judged to be linked to and motivated by social and economic imperatives with the corollary that if these conditions improved the attraction would fade.[53] The important question remains, however, how united were Saddam Hussein's opponents at that time? They clearly, were not a united monolithic body but rather a motley collection of 'mutually wary groups with differing objectives split between two main centres of activity – Damascus and Tehran'.[54] There can be no doubt about the ill-sorted nature of the opposition, the Damascus based DPNF and Tehran based Shi'a organization Da'wa (Islamic Call) which contracted a loose alliance with the mainstream Kurdish Democratic Party. One of the major problems of this two-pronged opposition, one secular, the other Islamist, was their mutual hostility. Also, their existence highlighted the regional dimension within Iraq's domestic political environment, i.e. Syria's bid to destabilize the Iraqi government and Iran meddling as part of its own quest for control, influence and theocratic aggrandizement. Citizen loyalty was a crucial factor in the maintenance of the state, particularly at a time of war. Doubts about the allegiance of the population could also be turned into an excuse for not introducing political reforms. As Saddam Hussein asserted in 1982: 'Iraq is too young for democracy. There are too many elements which reject the country.'[55] This statement carried a germ of truth, primordial affinities did render the country vulnerable to disintegration and appeared to justify, as much the same experience in other Third World states displays, a tendency towards governmental repression and brutality.

Saddam Hussein's views on democracy were always curious; never especially enamoured of the 'liberal democratic experience' on the grounds that it was developed and based on a capitalist mode of production, his understanding of democracy was uncompromising: 'We accept and will admit any discussion as long as the Arab Socialist Ba'ath Party remains the leader.'[56] With this working definition of democracy the roles of the new bodies, the National Assembly and the Legislative Council seem limited. In the elections in 1984 the Ba'ath Party won 73 per cent, that is, 183 of 250 seats and the president spoke of the 'new high standard for democracy' which indicated the Iraqi people's trust in a regime which was 'deep, stable and infallible'.[57]

Political reform

If Saddam Hussein was unlikely to be contradicted at home, perhaps more significantly he was not questioned abroad. Internationally, the war with

Iran marked the beginning of what many termed the 'honeymoon period' between Iraq and the United States, although America and the Soviet Union continued to trade arms with either Iraq or Iran, or both.[58] Neither superpower seemed greatly exercised by the Saddam Hussein regime and there were no calls for democracy in the 1980s, demands which were to become such a feature of the 1991 Gulf War. The president had undoubtedly strengthened his position during the war with Iran and consequently a greater concentration of power developed around his personal office at the expense of the RCC. Politically, it seemed encouraging when Hussein announced that a special committee would be set up to draft a new constitution which would allow for the formation of political parties.

Elections for the National Assembly, which had been continually postponed since the cease-fire on 18 July 1988 eventually took place in April 1989 on the grounds that 'it would provide more chances for those who want to stand'.[59] Presumably, encouraged by the exhortation to participate, some 42 candidates duly stood, only to find themselves barred by the RCC on the grounds of their alleged illiteracy.[60] All candidates were vetted by an election committee headed by the vice-chairman of the RCC. One quarter of the 953 candidates were members of the Ba'ath Party, 62 of whom were women. The remaining candidates were either independents or members of groupings affiliated to the National Progressive Front, which included the Kurdistan Democratic Party and the Kurdistan Revolutionary Party. More than half of the newly elected deputies declared themselves to be Ba'athists. The basic issue is why the matter of reform was raised. One possible reason might be on account of indigenous pressure, in that whilst people were prepared to make sacrifices during the war, they would definitely expect economic and political changes once the conflict ended.[61] Certainly, details of the proposed permanent constitution to be endorsed by the new assembly were radical: the executive body, the Council of Ministers would be responsible directly to the assembly; people would be free to form political parties, although the ICP would remain banned because of its support for Iran during the war. The possibility was also raised of the abolition of the RCC and the distribution of its powers among the National Assembly, the presidency and the Council of Ministers. The president would be elected directly by universal suffrage.[62]

The constitution, approved by the assembly, was published for 'public debate' in July 1990 and it was agreed that the president would be elected for an eight-year renewable term by direct elections and the RCC would be replaced by a consultative council with 50 members, half of whom would be appointed by the president, the rest by direct secret ballot. New political parties would be allowed, but only the Ba'ath party would be permitted to have branches in the armed forces and the police force. In many respects, these political moves could have been considered genuine shifts towards democratization had it not been for an event which took place only two days after the publication of the new constitution. On 2 August 1990, Iraq invaded Kuwait. This action set in train a series of

United Nations' resolutions and international responses which culminated in a war being fought against Iraq. In January 1992 a group of coalition forces led by the United States and largely funded by Kuwait and Saudi Arabia commenced an assault against Iraq.

Effects of 1991 Gulf War

It is not the purpose of this section to examine the process or conduct of the war. It will, however, consider the domestic political ramifications of the conflict. The invasion of Kuwait certainly stepped up political opposition. At a meeting in December 1990, in Damascus, an agreement was reached between 17 opposition groups belonging to the Iraqi National Joint Action Committee (INJAC) and a programme was produced which called for the overthrow of Saddam Hussein and the establishment of a democratic system. The agreement intended to bring to a formal end the long-standing differences between nationalist and Islamic opposition groups. The manifesto condemned the invasion of Kuwait and called for the immediate withdrawal of Iraqi forces. The formation of the Joint Action Committee may have come as a surprise to those who were not aware there were, in fact, 17 oppositionist groups. A consideration of *Table 4.2* reveals a rainbow coalition of almost staggering variety. Unquestionably united in their opposition to Saddam Hussein it would nevertheless, be difficult to estimate the degree of consensus which might be achieved on other political matters. Suddenly, oppositionist groups were appearing in numerous places, including two London-based organizations, which were non-INJAC members: the Nationalist Iraqi Constitution led by Salah Omar Ali and the Free Iraqi Congress, led by Saad Saleh Jaber. INJAC, nevertheless, issued a final statement calling for the development of an 'organisational and structural framework'; the establishment of a provisional government and the stipulation that once Saddam Hussein had been overthrown 'direct and free' elections would be held to a constituent council which would draw up a new constitution.

However, in June 1991 the Voice of the Iraqi Opposition radio reported the creation of a new organization, the Cadres of the Iraqi Islamic Da'wa Party, Middle East Branch. The party's main aim is the overthrow of Saddam Hussein and the establishment of a democratic regime which would return Iraq to 'its Arab and Islamic fold'. The organization rejects the policy of their leaders who associated with Iran, on the grounds that Da'wa's relationship with Iran 'has eclipsed Arab and international support for the Iraqi popular uprising in the south (Shi'a) out of fears that support will be a prelude to Iranian hegemony in the region'.[63] There is no doubt that a possible outcome on those lines has alarmed opinion in the West, but since the end of the war on 3 March 1991 there has been little certainty regarding the stability of Saddam Hussein's regime. There have been repeated reports of planned, attempted and failed coups by various military factions.[64] The divisions among the Iraqi army has led to speculation that military

Table 4.2 Members of the Iraqi National Joint Action Committee

Supreme Assembly of the Islamic Revolution of Iraq (SAIRI)
*Movement of the Iraqi Mujaheddin
*Islamic Movement in Iraq
*Al-Daawah al-Islamiyah
*Jund Al-Iman
*Islamic Action Organization
*Islamic Scholars Organization
Islamic Alliance
†Democratic Party of Kurdistan (DPK)
†Patriotic Union of Kurdistan (PUK)
†Kurdistan Socialist Party
†Kurdistan People's Democratic Party
Iraqi Communist Party
Dissident Ba'athists
Democratic Gathering
Iraqi Socialist Party
Independent Nationals

Source: *Keesings Record of World Events* 1991
Notes: *Member of SAIRI.
†Member of Kurdistan Iraqi Front along with Kurdish Socialist Party. Assyrian Democratic Party and Revolutionary Proletariat Kurdistan Party.

commanders could revolt at any moment. The Supreme Assembly of the Islamic Revolution in Iraq (SAIRI) leaders have distributed leaflets to army personnel in northern Iraq urging them to turn their weapons against Saddam Hussein and his clique.[65] In SAIRI's statement, outlining the shape of any future government it was emphasized that a government would be elected by secret ballot; all Iraqis would be treated equally, with religious beliefs, public freedoms and human rights respected. The government would also create good relations with its neighbours; honour all Arab, Islamic and international agreements and would no longer be a menace to other states.[66] SAIRI's intention to renew efforts to unite Iraqi opposition may prove difficult to achieve.

The Ba'athist newspaper, Al-Thawrah, announced in May 1991:

> Those who believe that democracy is purely Western-made seek to distort the truth. Those who believe it can be exported or that western democracy is the perfect human creation forget the fascist nature of this democracy and that colonialism has grown up and lived under its umbrella.[67]

The National Assembly endorsed the draft law on political parties in July 1991 and a few days later Saddam Hussein promised a new era of pluralism: 'Pluralism will be the main pillar of the next phase. I urge all nationalist Iraqis from all intellectual and political trends who are concerned with Iraq's sovereignty, unity and independence to turn a new page and forget the differences and contradictions of the past.'[68] The law, intended to 'legalise and organise political life in Iraq', carries stringent restrictions. Parties will be banned from carrying out 'any political indoctrination activities, or party organisation activities within the armed forces or police'. They will be dissolved if the Council of Ministers proves they have carried out activities 'threatening the state's security, territorial integrity, sovereignty, independence, and national unity', or if they 'encroach on the rights and freedoms of other parties'.[69] The 'new era of pluralism' seems to be a return to the political environment of the late 1980s.

Since the end of the 1991 war numerous commentators and analysts have considered the possibility of democratic advancement within Iraq. Some suggest that the invasion of Kuwait would never have taken place had Iraq been a functioning democracy, with opportunities for opposition.[70] Others are cheered by the fact that all main Iraqi political groupings, inside and outside the country 'raise slogans of democracy'.[71] Alternatively, others take a more pessimistic view, arguing that Iraq fulfils none of the most basic preconditions for democracy. The parties in exile are seen as distinct and largely unrepresentative bodies with ingrained differences. Democracy is associated with economic development, a sophisticated infrastructure and competent communications system, so damaged in Iraq during the two wars:

> Democracy is clearly meaningless if part of the population is below the poverty level and another part controls all the means of production. Moreover, since the majority of Kurdish and Iraqi population are very poor, notions of democracy are at best academic. It is, therefore, premature, not to say dangerous, to imagine that democracy is the panacea for Kurdish and Iraqi ills.[72]

There can, of course, be no fully informed discussion of the potentialities of Iraq's political system whilst Saddam Hussein remains president of the country and it is clear that the years of repression have exacted a price. When Saddam Hussein was announcing his new 'era of pluralism', one young person in Baghdad stated: 'I don't know anything about parties. I don't know anything about democracy.'[73] One factor, however, is clear, the rate at which political reform may or may not take place ultimately depends on the will of the Ba'ath Party.

Conclusion

As might be true of a number of artificially created states of the imperialist period, Iraq carried the essence of its own division and instability within its boundaries. Unreconciled and, indeed, possibly unreconcilable ethnic and religious differences within a nation-state raises a whole host of difficulties: conflict, secessionist tendencies, ideological rivalry, intemperate opposition and perhaps more damagingly, questions about citizen loyalty. The quest for unity and nation-state building has been one of the common features of the developing world, contributing to the agonized debate about the appropriateness of democracy or multi-partyism in such polarized polities. Some analysts, as was considered in Chapter 1, favoured the establishment of a strong one-party state, which could serve to unify the nation and harmonize social and economic discourse. With hindsight it is not an unreasonable assumption. After all how can there exist a pluralist political system within a country if vast sections of the population seek autonomy or separate development. Clearly, a multitude of fractious parties, unable to achieve agreement with other parties for very long and sometimes even arguing with each other is hardly conducive to stability or harmony. Yet in practice, the other side of the coin, the draconian authoritarian state under the control of a dominant party which penetrates all spheres of life and whose dispensations of justice are invariably brutal and arbitrary, is even less acceptable. The Ba'ath Party, as it operates in Iraq, is just such an example and its years of power have been tainted with violence and repression to Kurds, Shi'ites, communists and others. It is precisely the oppressive nature of authoritarian states which makes a balanced appraisal impossible and yet, one must be made. Has the Ba'ath Party contributed to political advancement in Iraq and if not, why not? Does the fault rest with the party or with the nation?

One enduring feature of the Ba'ath Party is that it is an organization indigenous to the region even if its ideology is partly divined from elsewhere. Consequently, it does possess a certain legitimacy in identifying, defending and preserving Arab dignity and integrity. It is, in other words, a home-grown party, unlike the local communist parties, who although unquestionably popular, received their instruction through Soviet directive. Communist parties, then, could not speak of the 'Arab Nation' with such clarity of meaning as could the Ba'ath Party, unharnessed by any affiliation to a foreign land. This factor was undoubtedly a profound source of strength yet ironically, during the Cold War period, its abiding weakness. If the Ba'ath Party were to be penetrated or used by a foreign power for purposes of superpower rivalry, the result could be extremely effective. During the Cold War era, there can be little doubt that the party's response to events mirrored those of the rival superpowers in that policies changed in rapid succession. First, the policy of brutality, partnership and then proscription for the indigenous communist party; second, the promises of reforms, pluralism and democracy which all remained unfulfilled; third, the new constitutional changes which were left untried and untested. These unsteadying policies were all combined with a seemingly cavalier attitude towards the Iraqi people.

Yet Iraq, in the form of considerable oil wealth, was granted a real opportunity to become a benevolent state, or at least a rentier state. Through the apportionment of welfare benefits, seemingly so successful in the Shi'ite community during the Iran–Iraq War, one step could have been taken towards pulling the nation together. Also a federal structure combining autonomy for the Kurdish peoples could have helped minimize tension. Primordial loyalties cannot be stamped out but have to be accommodated within a nation-state, if that state is to be preserved. As countries with ethnic and religious differences are many and varied, economic and social advance can be an effective way, if not of reducing heterogeneity, then at least of offering a different set of commonalities to link peoples together. The Ba'ath Party in Iraq, unlike its Syrian counterpart, seems to pay less regard to a 'socialist' ideology as such, but retains a firm belief in the notion of pan-Arabism, not of course, to be led by a Syrian-model Ba'athist state, but by the Iraqi variant. The Iraqi Ba'ath Party sees its role as one of regional leader at the expense of domestic amelioration. The years of the Iran–Iraq War contributed to the party's inflated notion of leading the 'Arab Nation' and in a sense, the invasion of Kuwait was one deluded step on the road towards achieving it. The country's quest for regional control may render it vulnerable to its neighbours in the post-war climate of the 1991 Gulf crisis but it has failed to diminish the potency of the Ba'ath Party. Opposition parties may form and unite, military coup attempts may be regular features but in the final analysis there is no indication that the Iraqi Ba'ath Party, under the stewardship of Saddam Hussein, has lessened its appetite for power. So what of political advancement under the party throughout its years in control? It has by default and through years of authoritarian rule given rise to the establishment of some form of alternative structure of government as witnessed by the meeting of a coalition of opposition groups at the Iraqi National Congress in Vienna in July 1992, even if such meetings are obliged to take place in the diaspora. If disparate groups can now reach a consensus about how Iraq should be governed there may develop a greater willingness to participate in democratizing processes. However, whether the Iraqi Ba'ath Party will ever relinquish power willingly is very much open to question.

The prospects for democratization in these dominant party states do not seem tremendously encouraging at the moment, but this is not to suggest that change cannot or, indeed, will not occur. As the recent radical political changes which took place within the old communist bloc were unforeseen, equally it is difficult to predict the political direction the two Ba'ath parties may take. However, one factor is absolutely definite, if moves towards democratization are made, via a changed or liberalizing leadership, as a result of indigenous or external pressure or simply because authoritarian states are no longer viewed as efficient or effective, both Syrian and Iraqi parties must be ready to accept their changed roles.

The multi-party state – Israel

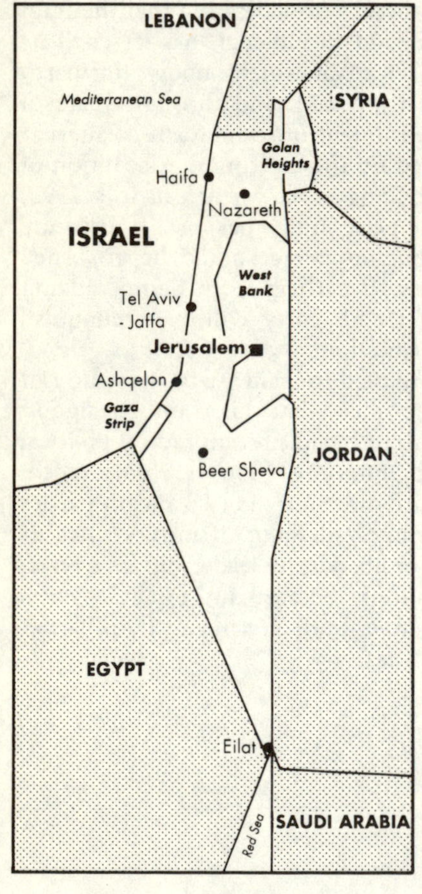

The creation of the State of Israel in 1948 had an enormous impact on the politics of the region. It was, of course, a genuinely 'new' state inasmuch as it was the result of the partitioning of Palestine and it might be argued that the difficulties confronting Israel were much the same as the problems facing any other new 'underdeveloped' nation: highly fluid social structure, tentative, provisional economic conditions and an abrupt transition to statehood. Yet there existed factors which were particular to Israel. One essential feature was the concept of Israel as a homeland for all Jewish people and the special conditions of its creation, following the Second World War and the holocaust, which resulted in the enormous influx of immigrants from Europe bringing with them political attitudes formed elsewhere. As Jehuda Reinharz states, the immigrants were:

> relatively unencumbered by the handicaps of a rigid local

> tradition. Thus, the establishment of new patterns of living rationally suited for adjustments to the social, cultural and economic, as well as political requirements of a modern nation in Palestine, was far easier for Israel than it was for the native Asian and African communities that acquired independence at the same time. A more suitable comparison would be those new nations of the Western Hemisphere that were colonized by immigrants from Europe.[1]

In 1948, 760,000 Jews lived in a state whose population expanded to over two million in a few years.[2] With such a disproportionate population balance between immigrant and indigenous population and with a 'right of return' law which encouraged Jewish people worldwide to live in Israel there would inevitably be a 'frontier' spirit among settlers who sought to contribute and identify with the well-being of the new state. In 1948, 598,000 Jews were living in Israel. Although, as Reinharz points out, large numbers of new immigrants came from countries unfamiliar with democratic government, certain organizations had existed during the British mandatory period, the Jewish Agency, the Histadrut (trade union federation) and other bodies, which, when statehood arrived, served to 'induct newcomers into advanced organizations'.[3] Clearly, then, the majority of the population of Israel from the moment of its creation had a very different cultural background and the nation largely defined its role as a 'settler state'.

Since 1948 and especially since the war of 1967, the dual questions of territorial control and the stateless Palestinian population have remained unresolved. Yet the impact of these problems has confronted Israel's political system. Although Israel regards itself as a liberal democracy and many view it as the only functioning multi-party pluralistic state in the Middle East, the problems of population mobility and subjugation can serve to undermine such a political structure. There have been occasions when policies which represent a clear abuse of rights, removal of civil liberties, or denial of political participation were approved and ratified in a seemingly democratic manner. Certainly, the factors which have affected the political advancement of other states in the region, shifting population and citizenship, have also had an impact on the developed polity of Israel thus showing that the distinction between developed, developing and underdeveloped states can be overstated. There is nothing innately 'Third World' about statelessness, population mobility, citizenship and the quest for civil and political rights, as has been evidenced recently by events in central and eastern Europe.

Yet the very creation of Israel was seen by the Arab community to be an act of imperialist intervention, since land was wrested from the Palestinian Arabs without agreement, and those peoples were displaced and continue to lack a sovereign state. The mobility of the Palestinians began in December 1947 barely a month after the United Nations partition resolution was passed, and continues to this day. Israel's right to exist as a nation-state was only recognized by the Palestine Liberation Organization (PLO) in 1988 and is still not fully acknowledged by a number of neighbouring Arab states. Under the British Mandate for Palestine the country was designated a Jewish homeland and the Jewish immigration facilitated by Britain at that time, fuelled Arab animosity towards the West in the post-colonial period. Certainly, the presence of the state of Israel is a major dynamic both in the area and within the domestic polities of the surrounding countries.

Finally, just as the superpower rivalry of the Cold War affected the other states in the region so too did it impinge on the political life of Israel. It was widely held for a long time, that as far as the United States was concerned, Israel could 'do no wrong', and was strategically necessary in a region which was becoming increasingly anti-Western. So in considering the case of Israel – and some might be inclined not to largely because 'few useful generalizations could be made that would apply with equal validity to Israel and to other countries in Middle East' – it is necessary to be judicious.[4] In fact, common issues do emerge, including questions of territorial control and expansion; regional and international pressures; the political implications of the ending of the Cold War; and most importantly, the impact wrought on Israel's political structures, of its policies towards the Palestinian Arabs in the occupied lands, but the effects are different. It must be remembered, then, that whilst Israel is distinct in cultural, religious and political terms its inclusion is essential to any understanding of the factors which affect democracy in the region.

The new state

Resolution 181 of the General Assembly of the United Nations, passed on 29 November 1947, recommended the partition, with economic union, of Palestine, into Arab and Jewish states. Palestine had been governed by Britain under a League of Nations Mandate since 1922 and upon British withdrawal, the Jewish state of Israel was declared. The Palestinian Arabs did not accept Resolution 181 and on 15 May 1948 the first Arab/Israeli war began. When Israel's boundaries were finally established by armistice agreements following the 1948/49 war, the state was one-fourth larger than had been designated under the United Nations resolution. Israel emerged occupying three-quarters of the territory of the mandated Palestine; of the remainder, the West Bank was annexed by Jordan in 1950 and the Gaza Strip passed to Egyptian administration whilst the Golan Heights came under Syrian control. As documented in Chapter 2 the creation of the state of Israel occasioned the mass exodus of Palestinian Arabs into the neighbouring Arab states. The 1967 Arab/Israeli war resulted in Israel capturing and occupying the West Bank, including East Jerusalem, Gaza, Sinai and the Golan Heights. In December 1981, Sinai was restored to Egypt under the terms of the Egypt–Israel Peace Treaty of March 1979 but the other areas have remained under Israeli occupation.

The Declaration of the Establishment of the State of Israel announced that the development of the country would be for the 'benefit of all its inhabitants and will be based on freedom, justice and peace . . . it will ensure complete equality of social and political rights to all its inhabitants irrespective of religion, race or sex; it will guarantee freedom of religion, conscience, language, education and culture'.[5] This Declaration is as relevant today as it was in 1948. Since 1967 Israel has occupied territories inhabited by some 1,530,000 Palestinian Arabs.[6]

It is internationally held that the Fourth Geneva Convention of 1949 relating to the Protection of Civilian Persons in Time of War, and regulations respecting the Laws and Customs of War on Land, annexed to the Hague Convention of 1907, apply to the occupied territories. Israel is regarded as having breached the legal instruments by changing the existing laws and rules of administration, settling her own population in occupied territory, deporting local inhabitants and violating individual human rights through collective punishments. Successive Israeli governments, however, have consistently stated that the Fourth Geneva Convention is not formally applicable to the territories on the following grounds: the fact that the occupation is not 'belligerent'; the extent of time which has elapsed since hostilities ended; and the absence of formal peace agreements. Israel maintains that the West Bank and Gaza are not 'enemy territory' as defined in the Convention and that the legal status of the territories is unique because Jordan's sovereignty over the West Bank was never internationally recognized and Egypt did not claim sovereignty over Gaza.

Nevertheless, whatever the claims and counter-claims, the occupied territories are widely considered to be the Achille's Heel of a country which is often portrayed as the only real democracy in the Middle East. Indeed, arguments have centred around policies pursued in the occupied territories and the very nature of democracy within Israel. One view suggests that actions in the West Bank and Gaza actually serve to undermine Israel's democracy.[7] Others maintain the occupation reveals the nation's political system to be:

> a false democracy. There is no such thing as a half-democracy; either democracy applies to all, or it applies to none. Among Jewish Israelis there is freedom of speech; of the press and of association. However, the Palestinians are deprived of their civil and political rights. This is a false democracy.[8]

Certainly, the connection has not escaped the notice of former leader of the Israeli Labour Party, Shimon Peres, who cautioned against Israel becoming 'eternal border policemen in Gaza where we fight and patrol', which ultimately would endanger the nation as a 'national and democratic state'.[9] If Israel attempts to reassure itself in the belief that at least it has a democracy to undermine, there can be no doubt that the territories have had a direct and penetrating impact on the political complexion of the country.

Political structures

Israel has no written constitution. In June 1950 the parliament, the Knesset, voted to adopt a state constitution by evolution over an unspecified period. As such, a series of laws have been passed, including the Law of Return (1950), the Law of Equal Rights for Women (1951), and the Basic Law (1958) which defines the structure and procedure of the Knesset. The Knesset has 120 members elected by general, equal, secret and proportional elections every four years. Every Israeli national over the age of 18 years, including the small Arab population within Israel proper, is enfranchised. The President possesses no power to veto legislation and the courts cannot declare any law passed by the Knesset to be unconstitutional.

Israel's electoral system follows an advanced pattern and has been regarded as approaching the 'purest form of proportional representation'.[10] The principles regarding the Knesset elections, set out in Article 4 of the Basic Law, ensure that the whole country serves as a single national constituency. At elections, voters do not vote for individual candidates but for party lists; all voters in the whole country having the same lists before them. They can only vote for the lists as produced with no alterations. There are no by-elections and should any vacancy occur the position is filled by the next name on the party list.[11] The system is accessible for any group of 750 Israelis eligible to vote, who may submit a list and, of course, the process encourages small groups to seek election. It is the very nature of the electoral system, that is, the basic proportional list system in conjunction with its 1 per cent threshold, which has been criticized as instrumental in leading to problems of 'immobilism and fragmentation' which became a feature of Israel's party system throughout the 1980s.[12]

Although attempts at electoral reform have been considered at various intervals since the 1950s none has been implemented mainly because an increase in the threshold, even to say 3 per cent, would effectively eliminate any party with less than four Knesset seats. On the 1988 electoral returns, a total of eight parties would not have been eligible to sit in parliament: Mapan, Techiya, Tsomet, Moledet, Shinui, the progressive List for Peace, the Arab Democratic Party and Degal HaTora.[13] To some observers such a move would be beneficial in eliminating splinter groups who are seen to wield excessive power in relation to their electoral support, particularly when they participate in shaky coalition governments. Alternatively, such a low threshold could be seen to be truly democratic in that no group, however small, is prevented from parliamentary participation. Debate of this kind invariably centres on the efficacy of coalition governments and the deals the majority party is obliged to make with small and often more extremist parties. The results of such associations effectively immobilize the larger party of government. There is nothing new in these arguments but the significant aspect of Israeli politics is the fact that all parties and groupings have a position on the territorial issue. Indeed, some of the ultra-nationalist parties, Tsomet, Techiya and Morasha, with their 'not one inch' approach to any negotiations regarding territory, have gained notoriety largely because of their inflexible policies. This factor makes their participation in a coalition government particularly problematic. The effects of the country's political system reverberates on the lives and possible life chances of Palestinian Arabs in the occupied territories. Electoral politics and the relative advantages of differing forms of proportional representation are no longer the preserves of dry academic debate but a fundamental element in a democracy's ability to deal with crises of its own making.

Cultural/religious factors

If the peoples who emigrated from Europe, America and other parts of the world in the early years of the state possessed a settler mentality in wanting to build a new homeland they also had a long memory of the historical oppression of the Jewish race. If they could develop and structure advanced forms of political expression they also had the potential for conquest as a means of defence. The defence of Jewish people could be articulated politically through territorial control legitimized by the hostility of neighbouring Arab states. According to Haim Baram, an Israeli writer, the wide assortment of political groups and parties ranging from the social democratic to the arch-religious and radically extremist fall into specific categories defined by different interpretations of the protection of the state. The categories are: the *massada syndrome;* the *fundamental expansionist;* the *pragmatic expansionist;* the *doves* and the *peace camp.*[14]

The *massada syndrome* produces a political outlook which is predominantly bleak and fatalistic, bordering almost on xenophobia.[15] Historically, the non-Jewish world has inflicted cruelties on Jewish peoples and the Arabs are largely seen as enemies. The nature of the Arab/Israeli conflict is defined by mutual exclusion and racial identity. Greater Israel should occupy the entire Mandated territory which is an objective derived from Zionism. This view is shared by some members of the Techiya, the Moledet and Tsomet parties and the National Religious Party. *Fundamental expansionists* also adhere to the Greater Israel view but mainly rationalize it with the need for Israel to maintain adequate security against potential aggression from the Arab states. The position is defended on the grounds that Israel's right to exist is still not accepted by some Arab nations and therefore, a prospective state of belligerency is constantly threatened. This view was strengthened immediately after the Gulf War when it was perceived that without the occupied territories, Israel would be placed in the same position as Kuwait, vulnerable to invasion. Thus there could be 'no move to pre-1967 borders'.[16] No population transfer is envisaged in maintaining the territorial status quo and a significant number of Likud and some Labour Members of Knesset (MKs) support this position. The *pragmatic expansionists*, on the other hand, accept the possibility of a partial Israeli withdrawal from the West Bank and some form of 'territorial compromise'. Jordan, in the past, has been cited as a likely participant in negotiations, and may well be in the future. As the occupied territories were gained because of Israel's defensive measures, should a situation prevail in which a peace settlement was achieved, the Pragmatic Expansionists would readily consider it. The 'Land for Peace' proposals of the 1980s were perused seriously by adherents of this category who tend to be predominantly Labour MKs.

The *doves*, as might be suspected, reject much of the settlement policy in the West Bank, fearing the brutalizing effect on Israeli society such a long occupation of the territories might entail. Moderate Arab peace initiatives are often welcomed although there has been uncertainty in regard to their responses and possible contacts with the PLO. The dove category is continually critical of any oppressive measures which may occur in the territories, such as, harsh treatment of the indigenous population, arrests, deportations, and so on, but the position is vulnerable to charges of lack of patriotism. The inability to confront these accusations has somewhat weakened its position in the past. However, a small number of Labour MKs fall into this category as do a few Mapan MKs and in January 1990 the contradictions of this position came into sharp focus. A political crisis centred on the figure of Ezer Weizmann, the Minister of Science and Technology, former Likud member but latterly part of the Labour camp, and the leading 'Dove' in the cabinet. Evidence relating to Weizmann's PLO contacts was revealed by the prime minister when he alleged that Israel's internal security service, Shin Bet, had monitored a telephone conversation between Weizmann and a Palestinian activist. There had also been a meeting with a PLO representative. Prime Minister Shamir announced his intention to dismiss Weizmann and although the Labour Party opposed such a move, it was careful not to defend Weizmann. The situation became especially sensitive when Weizmann revealed that it was the Labour leader and vice-prime minister, Shimon Peres, who had actually briefed him during his telephone conversation with the Palestinian. Weizmann eventually resigned but the obvious deception involved, the ambiguity surrounding Peres' role and the government's judgement that any contact with the PLO was a heinous crime, highlighted the constraints of a position which was deemed to be treacherous. However, there is considerable mobility between the Doves and the final category, the Peace Camp, who advocate an Israeli withdrawal from all the occupied territories including East Jerusalem and who strive for formal negotiation between the government and the PLO. *Peace camp* supporters uphold the Palestinian right to self-determination and consider the establishment of an independent Palestinian state alongside Israel as the best possible solution to the Middle East conflict.

These categories, although neither immutable nor exhaustive provide a compact summary of the various positions and fluidity of party allegiances. However, such neat classifications mask the fact that cleavages between and within party organizations are profound and potentially destabilizing. After less than fifteen months in power, Israel's 'National Unity' coalition government collapsed in March 1990. The reasons for the breakdown were the fundamental differences between coalition partners over 'the pace and direction of the Middle East peace process'.[17] The government had been riven by the issue of the occupied territories but this time the splits were not simply between parties but actually within them. This instance of inter- and intra-party division revealed the capacity of the issue to influence both the way in which a government was elected and the manner in which it met its demise. Admittedly, the 'peace process' which was being conducted by the then US Secretary of State, James Baker, exerted pressure on the Shamir government. Baker demanded a quick Israeli response to a number of unresolved issues which Shamir found increasingly separated him from his own party. The contention ultimately led to five Likud MKs announcing the establishment of a separate party, the Party for the Advancement of Zionist Ideology in protest at Shamir's leadership. This move brought down the government on a vote of no confidence and the whole question of peace talks was put into abeyance.

One of the major features of the Israeli political system which has received considerable attention in recent years has been the apparent rightward drift of the electorate. This tendency has been evident since 1977, the year in which the Labour Party lost the political pre-eminence it had held since 1948. Studies revealed an ethnic dimension to voting behaviour in 1977. An 'important key to the upsurge of the Likud Party', was that the party won greater support from Israelis born of Oriental parentage.[18] The linkage between 'Oriental' or 'Sephardic' Jews and a more 'hawkish' and uncompromising stance with regard to the Palestinian Arabs, has been established in their voting behaviour. Such preferences have led some analysts to examine the linkage more closely and to differentiate between non-Ashkenazi Jews, those of non-European/North American extraction and their electoral predilections.[19] Israel Shahak suggests in Table 5.1 that a reversed pattern emerges when comparing Iraqi with Moroccan and Tunisian community party preferences, in that a greater proportion of the Iraqi community voted for Labour, whereas the Moroccan and Tunisian communities favoured Likud. However, as Table 5.2 reveals the actual size of the communities is extremely important. It is clear from this second table that significant differences exist in the sizes of the respective communities residing in Israel and therefore relative voting percentages will have a varied impact on the outcome of elections. Indeed, in towns which have a predominantly homogeneous population such as, Netivot, a Morrocan Jewish town, or Rosh Ha'ain which is of Yemenite descension, landslide victories occur for the right of centre and religious parties. In the 1981 elections, it was in towns such as these that Likud, the religious parties and the Techiya Party, between them, attracted 90 per cent of the vote.[20]

Table 5.1 Community voting in Israel

Community	*Votes for Labour alignment* %	*Votes for Likud* %	*All others* %
Polish	60	31	9
Russian	62	29	6
Romanian	80	14	6
Iraqi	54	39	7
Yemenite	31	53	16
Moroccan and Tunisian	18	67	15

Note: A community here includes those born in Israel
Source: *Middle East International*, 15 June 1984

Table 5.2 Jewish communities in Israel

Jewish communities in Israel	*000s*
Morocco (with Tangiers)	472.2
Tunisia and Algeria	120.1
Yemen and South Yemen	164.7
Iraq	268.3
Turkey	93.0
Egypt and Sudan	67.2
Bulgaria and Greece	67.1
Iran	118.7
Russia	293.8
Poland	322.3
Romania	285.6
Germany and Austria	93.3

Source: *Middle East International*, 15 June 1984

It is perhaps a mark of the 'settler' community and a feature of the right of return that racial origin should become an important political factor. The concept of 'Sephardic' Jews was an Ashkenazi one and did not stem from the 'oriental' community, but any country whose population is drawn from varied nations in different continents, all with a multitude of political traditions, will find those differences reflected in political patterns. Since the end of the Cold War there have been 400,000 immigrants enter Israel, mostly from the Soviet Union and although it is too early to predict where their political affinities might rest, their presence is a new dynamic for the country's electoral system.

Parties/elections

There is a wide diversity of opinion on the territorial question within political parties. As Table 5.3 indicates, proposed solutions to the Palestinian problem run on a continuum from recommended negotiations with the

PLO to an annexation of the West Bank and Gaza and population transfer. These views are widely canvassed across the country and have an inevitable impact on the direction of people's voting behaviour. According to David Capitanchik, the 1988 election campaign, although ostensibly about the Intifada, the uprising in the occupied territories which began in December 1987, and the immobilism of the government was, in fact, concerned with the so-called 'hidden agenda', that of the 'demographic timebomb'. The 'timebomb' was a new way of describing an old problem: majorityhood-versus-minorityhood of the Jewish population in Israel. In early post-mandate days this problem centred on the Arab population within Israel, now it focuses on the higher birthrate among the Arabs. The demographic issue has always been an emotive one and when Capitanchik refers to a 1988 opinion poll survey in which 97 per cent of respondents believe it necessary to retain the Jewish nature of the state, it barely differs from the first prime minister of Israel, David Ben-Gurion's statement in 1947: 'There could be no stable and strong Jewish state so long as it has a Jewish majority of only 60%.'[21]

One of the arguments used by Israeli opponents of Prime Minister Begin's Jewish settlement policies in the West Bank in the early 1980s was precisely that insidious annexation would create a situation by the year 2000 of eventual Arab majorityhood in Israel and the occupied territories, chiefly on account of the predicted increase in the Arab birthrate. As attractive as the occupied territories are to many Israelis there is the fundamental problem of the Arab population which continually gives the lie to former prime minister, Golda Meir's famous claim that 'the Palestinians do not exist'.[22] It was also stated by Shimon Peres more recently in 1991 that 'Annexing the territories (means) annexing the residents as well'.[23]

For certain political groups, however, the argument inexorably moves to its logical conclusion: if the land is wanted but the indigenous population is not, an obvious solution emerges – population transfer. During the 1988 election the idea of 'transfer' of the Arab population in the occupied territories began to be discussed more openly. Indeed, a survey revealed that 60 per cent of potential supporters for the Likud and parties further to the right supported 'transfer'.[24] The share of Knesset seats won by Moledet, Techiya and Tsomet in their grouping increased from five to seven (see Table 5.4). In a parliament of 120 members these figures seem less than significant yet they were to form part of the Likud leader, Yitzhak Shamir's new coalition, along with the orthodox religious block which comprised 16 members: six Shia (Sephardi Orthodox), 5 National Religious Party, 5 Agudut Yisrael. The Moledet Party's platform declared its position in favour of population 'transfer' and although the religious parties were not quite so extreme they were disposed to the 'Greater Israel' position with possibly the annexation of the West Bank and Gaza, as well as the introduction of a more rigorous form of Judaism.

The importance of these groups, small but influential when balancing a coalition, has been recognized by Likud and Labour. Both major parties

Table 5.3 Israel's political parties

Political party	*Type of party*	*Solution to the Palestinian problem*
HADASH (Formerly Rakach) (Communists) Democratic Front for Peace and Equality	Communist Marxist-Leninist	Two states solution
MEKADEMET SHALOM Progressive List for Peace (PLP)	More nationalist orientated than Hadash	Two states solution. Negotiate with PLO
MAPAM United Workers Party	Socialist Zionist	Land for Peace and Israeli-Palestinian-Jordanian Confederation. Negotiate with PLO if renounce terror
RATZ Citizens Rights Movement	Civil Rights Group	Israeli-Palestinian-Jordanian Confederation. Peace with security arrangements.
MARACH Labour Alignment (main components Mapai-Israel Labour Party and Yachad, Ezer Weizmann's Party)	Democratic Socialist	Israeli-Palestinian-Jordanian Confederation. Continuation of status quo: No Palestinian state
CENTRE PARTY New amalgamation of Shinui, Independent Liberals and Liberal Centre Party	Liberal	Palestinian-Jordanian Confederation; continuation status quo

LIKUD Herut, Liberals, Ometz, and La'am.	Nationalist	Continuation of status quo. Autonomy for Palestinians
MAFDAL National Religious Party	Religious – Zionist	Continuation of status quo. 'Greater Israel'
AGUDAT YISRAEL	Ashkenazi Ultra-orthodox	Continuation of status quo maybe annexation of West Bank and Gaza
SHAS Sephardi Torah Guardians	Sephardi Ultra-orthodox	Continuation of status quo maybe annexation of West Bank and Gaza
TSOMET	Ultra-nationalist	'Not one inch approach'. 'Greater Israel'. Annexation of West Bank and Gaza Strip
TECHIYA	Ultra-nationalist	'Not one inch approach'. 'Greater Israel'. Annexation of West Bank and Gaza Strip
MORASHA	Religious Ultra-nationalist	'Not one inch approach'. 'Greater Israel'. Annexation of West Bank and Gaza Strip
MOLEDET	Ultra-orthodox Ultra-nationalist	'Drive the Palestinians out'. 'Greater Israel'. Annexation of West Bank and Gaza Strip

Table 5.4 General election results

	Percentage		Seats	
	1988	*1984*	*1988*	*1984*
Consolidation (Likud)	31.1	(31.9)	40	(41)
Labour Party (Ma'arach)*	30.0	(34.9)	39	(38)
Sephardic Torah Guardians (Shas)	4.7	(3.1)	6	(4)
National Religious Party (Mafgal)	3.9	(3.5)	5	(4)
Union of Israel (Agudat Israel)	4.5	(1.7)	5	(2)
Civil Rights and Peace Movement (Ratz)	4.3	(2.4)	5	(3)
Democratic Front (Hadash)	3.7	(3.4)	4	(4)
Zionist Revival Movement (Techiya)†	3.1	(4.0)	3	(4)
United Workers' Party (Mapam)*	2.5	–	3	(6)
Renewed Zionist Party (Tzomet)†	2.0	–	2	(1)
Homeland (Moledet)	1.9	–	2	–
Centre-Change (Merkaz-Shinui)	1.0	(2.6)	2	(3)
Torah Flag (Degel Hatorah)	1.5	–	2	–
PLP	1.5	(1.8)	1	(2)
Arab Democratic Party	1.2	–	1	–
Others	3.1	(10.7)	0	(8)

**Mapam* contested 1984 election on joint list with Labour.
†Tzomet contested 1984 election on joint list with *Techiya*.

Source: *Keesings Record of World Events*, Vol. 35, No. 9.

have courted these organizations in attempts to forge broad-based coalitions. Despite protestations it was reported in 1990 that Labour had signed an agreement with the Ultra-Orthodox party, Agudat Yisrael in an attempt to form a government. The agreement indicated that Labour had undertaken to halt the legislative process for a Bill of Rights and had willingly complied with restrictive religious measures.[25] At that time Peres failed to achieve a majority despite this element of horse-trading; Agudat Yisrael withdrew support from Labour at the last moment. It was then Likud's turn to try to form a new government and the process repeated itself once again. This unedifying spectacle of Labour and Likud desperately bidding for support among the smaller parties and factions aroused dissatisfaction in the media and among the public with Israel's electoral system which facilitated such practices. In 1990 approximately 150,000 demonstrators marched through Tel Aviv in support of electoral reform.

The political polarization within Israeli society is not in doubt and perhaps it truly is the mark of a real democracy to have a system of proportional representation which reflects this lack of uniformity. Yet in a country such as Israel, with undefined borders and a subjugated population in the occupied territories the paradox of democracy is stark. The niceties of an excessively democratic electoral process are sharply contrasted with the plight of the virtually disenfranchised peoples living in the occupied areas of the West Bank and Gaza. If democracy is to be more than an elaborate electoral system; if it is to avoid being condemned as neither just nor fair, questions of territorial control and occupation must be confronted.

Policies in occupied territories

In certain respects Israel's military success of the 1967 Six Day War could be judged to be a Pyrrhic victory especially with regard to the international opprobrium Israel has incurred over its occupation of the territories. Although, it is true that 90 per cent of territory gained during that conflict was returned to Egypt as a result of the Camp David Accords in 1979, the fact that only 10 per cent remains has done little to diminish concern and, indeed, has focused attention on Israel's policies in those areas. The West Bank and Gaza District, since 1967, have both been administered by Israel under a system of military government. Although Jordanian law remains in force in the West Bank, despite Jordan's severance of legal and administrative ties in July/August 1988, these are augmented and at times supplanted by Israeli military regulations, East Jerusalem was reunified with West Jerusalem on 26 June 1967, when the Knesset passed legislation which placed the whole area under Israeli sovereignty. According to Israel's Basic Law, Jerusalem complete and unified, is the capital of Israel. Five months after the Six Day War, the United Nations expressed its concern, asserting the 'inadmissability of the acquisition of territory by war and the need to work for a just and lasting peace in which every state in the area can live in security'. Resolution 242, proclaimed on 22 November 1967 called for:

1 The withdrawal of Israeli armed forces from territories occupied in the recent conflict.
2 Termination of all claims or states of belligerency and respect for and acknowledgement of the sovereignty, territorial integrity and political independence of every state in the area and their right to live in peace within secure and recognized boundaries free from threats or acts of force.

It further affirmed the necessity:

1 of guaranteeing freedom of navigation through international waterways in the area;
2 of achieving a just settlement of the refugee problem;
3 of guaranteeing the territorial inviolability and political independence of every state in the area, through measures including the establishment of demilitarized zones'.

The occupation has raised several questions about the nature of policies pursued by democratic states. The usual claim that democracies, unlike dictatorships, are restrained in their policies by their obligation to take account of public opinion may be re-examined. It is clear that democracies can actually permit the seizure of land through an act of war and the retention of that land by dignifying the process with the claim that it is vital for the nation's security. The wider question is whether or not a democracy can function if territorial boundaries are uncertain and people are living under occupation. In the 1970s Israel commended itself on exercising

> less control over the residents of the West Bank than it is legally entitled to do. Under international law, the life of the local population could be extremely restricted. In practice, this does not happen. Israel tries, in a spirit of good will, even when it would be very much easier not to do so. The result is that the West Bank Arabs operate in an atmosphere of freedom which is not tolerated in any Arab country.[26]

Israel has also outlined the various civil liberties to which Palestinian Arabs are entitled: freedom of expression, in that meetings, printing and publishing and marches are permitted; complete religious freedom; freedom of the press with Arab newspapers permitted to criticize the Israeli government; the right to strike and freedom of movement into and out of Israel. However, the picture of stability and contentment which these views portray does not correspond to reality especially since the Intifada began in December 1987. Over 800 Palestinians and some 40 Israelis have died in the unrest which has had a debilitating effect on both sides. Uprisings and demonstrations in the occupied territories were not, however, a new phenomenon. The Intifada, coordinated by the Unified National Command of the Uprising (UNCU) and including PLO representatives, gained momentum fed initially on deep resentment and frustration towards Israel and latterly by Israel's heavy-handed response to the Palestinians. There is no doubt that the Intifada resulted in punishing reactions from Israel which impinge beyond security measures into the sphere of civil rights. The Military Advocate-General announced in October 1989 that since the beginning of the Intifada, 86 Israeli soldiers and officers had been tried in military courts on charges such as violence, unjustified shooting and manslaughter, while 40,000 Arab residents had been detained since December 1967 and 18,000 charged.

International organizations have been alerted to Israeli actions in the territories and an Amnesty International Report published in January 1990 noted that the guidelines on the use of firearms had been progressively extended during the Intifada. The report expressed concern that the guidelines appeared to permit the unjustifiable killing of people who were involved in activities not necessarily endangering life.[27] A further Amnesty International Report published in August 1991 accused the Israeli government of continuing to endorse 'interrogation practices which amount to torture or ill-treatment, despite repeated protests from international human rights organizations'.

The pattern of torture, Amnesty claims, is clear throughout the occupied territories: detainees are 'systematically hooded with dirty sacks and deprived of food or sleep, usually by being shackled in painful positions while held in solitary confinement.[28] Although the Intifada was seen to be as much a 'protest against the state of affairs within Palestinian society as it was a revolt against Israeli occupation', many felt it was inadvisable for Israel to keep the Palestinians in line through measures of repression.[29]

The 1991 Gulf War

The Gulf War temporarily shifted international opinion in favour of Israel. And yet as soon as the aerial bombing of Iraq began on the night of 16/17 January, the Israeli authorities imposed a strict curfew throughout the occupied territories the purpose of which was to prevent Palestinians from intensifying the Intifada, and supposedly thereby indicating support for Iraq. A report issued in February 1991 by the Israeli Human Rights group, B'tselem, claimed that the effects of the curfew threatened the 'health, livelihood and welfare' of the Palestinians.[30] It claimed that 3650 people had been arrested during the curfew and that the Israeli authorities had distributed only 50,000 gas masks to protect against possible Iraqi chemical attack, among a Palestinian population of 1,700,000. However, the general mood of the time, certainly internationally and among some Arab states, was that the PLO and Yasser Arafat had committed a grave error in openly supporting Iraq throughout the war. Palestinians, as a consequence, became as much of a security risk in the Arab state of Kuwait, as in the Jewish state of Israel.

The Gulf War was widely interpreted as greatly damaging to the Palestinian cause in that it discredited the PLO and moved the focus of attention away from Israeli policies in the occupied territories. Israel's refusal to engage in military reprisal when under Iraqi Scud missile attack presented a responsible image and Opinion Poll Surveys conducted in the country in January and February 1991, suggested a continued commitment to democracy. A quarter of those interviewed still favoured the return of the territories to the Palestinians, a remarkable number given that Iraq fired a total of 39 Scud missiles at Israel between 18 January and 25 February resulting in one death and 200 casualties (see Table 5.5). It is the more remarkable since members of the government were cautioning that had a Palestinian state existed, Saddam Hussein would be attacking Israel from the West Bank.[31] By November 1991, an opinion poll revealed that 74 per cent would sanction the surrender of the West Bank and Gaza in return for an agreed peace.[32] The polls clearly indicated the existence of a body of opinion within the country which was uneasy with Israel's territorial policies. A month earlier thousands had turned out for a rally in Tel Aviv calling on the government to make concessions in the pursuit of peace.

These views were not reflected in the actions and statements of the Likud government, settlements continued in the occupied territories and Prime Minister Shamir spoke of the West Bank and Gaza as 'part of the land of Israel', on which it was intended to 'settle a multitude of Jews'.[33] According to the West Bank Data Project, an independent Israeli research group, over

Table 5.5 Israeli opinion poll surveys

	January 1991 %	*February 1991* %
Opposed to restrictions on democracy	43	60
In favour of equal rights for all	62	67
Support negotiations with PLO	53	44
In favour of returning territories to Arabs	30	26

Source: V. Bogdanor, 'Israeli Political Attitudes', London School of Economics, University of London, 26 June 1991

50 per cent of land on the West Bank and 40 per cent of that in Gaza had been placed under direct Israeli control, expropriated for settlements or set aside for other purposes, including military training areas. By April 1991 the controversial issue of Israeli settlements once again became the subject of intense domestic and international debate. A US State Department report to Congress stated that over 200,000 Israeli settlers were living in some 200 settlements in the occupied territories and of those 185,000 Soviet Jews who emigrated to Israel during 1990, around 4 per cent had settled in the territories. The American administration was particularly interested in the affair because it had signed a guarantee for a loan to Israel for the housing of new immigrants on the strict understanding that the funds would not be used for settlements in the territories. By 1992 the US made clear that the US$10 billion in loan guarantees would not be made available to the Likud government despite claims that in the post-Gulf War environment, the settlements provided Israel with 'strategic depth'.[34] With an election due in the summer of 1992 some analysts felt that America had overstepped the mark and was now meddling in internal politics. Certainly Secretary of State James Baker made a pointed statement: 'The choice is Israel's. She can determine whether she wants to take action which will permit the strong support for these loan guarantees or not.'[35] As Yitzhaq Rabin the new leader of the Labour Party was stressing the importance of making peace now that the International Middle East conference had been established and promising no more settlements it is perhaps not surprising that the Labour Party won the general election. Yet it must be remembered that Rabin, only three months before the election spoke of the need to establish autonomy for the Palestinians within 'nine months' of gaining office.[36] Given that a new configuration exists in the Middle East in the post-Gulf war period, with the US forming a defence pact with Kuwait, enlarging its military presence in the region and clearly no longer so reliant on the political or strategic asset of Israel, reform may be embraced. There can be no doubt that with the end of the Cold War possibilities are raised

of a change of policy but maybe more importantly, Israel now has a leader who refers to the 'mad delusion of Greater Israel and policies of political settlements'.[37] There may now be sufficient political will to deal squarely with these issues before Israel's policy of occupation and control profoundly erode the country's democratic base.

Conclusion

The creation of Israel set in train a series of events which have almost become institutionalized problems of the Middle East: the plight of Palestinian refugees; the occupation of land; the mutual hostility of Arab and Jew, the recurrent wars and conflicts and the general feeling that these issues would remain unresolved. During the Cold War period this was a pretty accurate interpretation. The further America involved itself in talks in the region the greater the suspicion in Soviet quarters and Arab client states that it was motivated by considerations of strategic and military advantage. In this political climate Israel was something of a hostage to fortune: desperately dependent on financial assistance from the United States but further encouraged in regional belligerency. These policies were exacerbated by superpower rivalry but, and this is an important point, they were also partly conditioned by the nature of Israel's creation and demography; arguments about the Jewish lobby in the American Congress could find echoes in the kith-and-kin debates in Britain about Rhodesia in the 1960s, or attitudes towards the policies of South Africa some years ago. In other words, the policies of these 'settler' states arouse a different response from the West than would the adoption of similar policies by, say, the indigenous governments of Nigeria or Ghana. This incidentally calls into question the assumption that the old 'primordial loyalties' are a feature only of 'traditional' societies, for it is precisely those cultural and societal bonds which serve to link the West with former 'settler' colonies irrespective of the draconian nature of policies pursued by respective governments.

Another factor is that whilst Israel's political structure is vastly different from its neighbours it is comparable with those of a number of European states and is regarded by many as a classic example of a liberal democratic state and a model for other 'developing' nations. There can be no question that Israel's electoral system is advanced and highly democratic, presenting the voter with a vast array of choice at election times. Yet, the core aspects which traditionally define statehood, territorial boundary and population/citizenship, are unclear. As the role of population mobility, citizen loyalty and the granting of political and civil rights have been of such overwhelming significance in the political structures of a number of states in the Middle East, affecting their ability to introduce policies of reform, so too do these issues present Israel with a profound challenge. States with shifting or subjugated populations corralled in occupied territory and denied appropriate rights, render the nation vulnerable both internally and externally. Equally, a policy of control and expropriation of land, irrespective of any military rationale will not endure indefinitely without brutalizing damage being inflicted on the population and increasing levels of repression having to be introduced to stem opposition. Violence breeds more violence on this downward spiral of political efficacy. Nevertheless, it is encouraging to note that even at the most crucial times of war and conflict, a significant sector of public opinion within the country has supported restoring land to the Palestinians, irrespective of government policy.

Israel, of course, does not fit the picture of the Third World state struggling against dictatorship and control and engaging in unsuccessful attempts at democracy. It has a more advanced political structure than many Western countries. It is a politically developed multi-party, pluralistic state but it has pursued policies for which any authoritarian state would be condemned. It may now be the moment in this changed international climate after the Cold War and the 1991 Gulf War, and given the new perspective of the government, for a real change to occur. After all, the dual questions of territory and population may prevent a country from democratizing but they can also severely undermine a democratic state. Consequently, Israel cannot be omitted from a study of democracy in the Middle East, simply on the grounds that the country has a multi-party system of government and does not approximate the general 'model' of political behaviour in the region. The policies and responses of Israel have a profound impact on the domestic political processes of a number of states in the area and maybe, more significantly, the issues which trouble those states also undermine Israel's pluralistic system.

The confessional state – the Lebanon

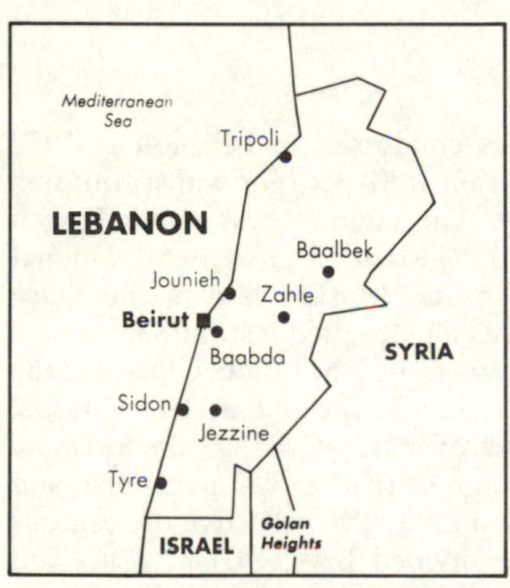

The political experience of Lebanon in recent years has revealed its profound vulnerability to the actions of neighbouring states and regional political organizations, providing at times an empirical illustration of Huntington's characterization of national disintegration and political decay: a society 'lacking law, authority, cohesion, discipline and consensus, where private interests dominate public ones, where there is an absence of civic obligation and civic duty and where political institutions are weak and social forces strong'.[1] Yet it was not so long ago that the country was commended by political scientists as a model of democracy largely absent from the Middle Eastern states. As discussed in Chapter 1, Lijphart referred to the political system of Lebanon as an example of the consociational model of government. Such a process was considered to be a more appropriate form of democracy, largely on account of its perceived steadying capacities in countries ethnically or religiously divided. The consociational framework, then, was expressed in Lebanon's confessional system of government which attempted to balance the interests of various groups by differentiation on religious lines. Indeed, Lebanon had prided itself on its democratic environment which sought to maintain a semblance of equity within its diverse population, and claims were made that within the country 'democracy and freedom are indispensable ingredients for a stable political system'.[2]

So what happened in Lebanon and was it an inevitable consequence of the juggling of different interests on confessional lines? One writer suggests: 'The religious antagonisms, the cultural divide, the weakness of government have all been apparent for decades. They made Lebanon what it was: a country with no unity, a country without a sense of nationhood, a country whose citizens were loyal not to the state but to their religious communities.'[3] If this was, in fact, the case it is surprising the country's political system lasted as long as it did, nearly thirty years. It is necessary, then, to consider the pre-war Lebanese political structure, the political fall-out during the civil war and the recently introduced constitutional changes in order to assess the extent to which democracy has been, is and will be a continuing feature of Lebanese political culture. As with other case studies certain factors emerge as significant determinants of political direction, namely, external pressures of a regional rather than a Cold War complexion, communal division, and the political implications of the ending of the 1991 Gulf War.

Political structure

According to the latest and only census conducted in Lebanon in 1932 Christians form a majority of the population at 52 per cent whilst Muslims represent 45.5 per cent (see Table 6.1). The country was under French mandate at the time and it was not until 1943 that an unwritten 'National covenant' was agreed between Christian and Muslim leaders and independence was gained. The National Covenant allocated institutional power between religious groups: the president was to be a Maronite Christian; the prime minister a Sunni Muslim; the speaker of the unicameral National Assembly a Shi'a Muslim and the chief of staff of the armed forces, a Druze. On the basis of the census it was agreed that seats in parliament and administrative positions would be allotted on a ratio reflective of religious affiliations, that is, positions would be divided between Christians and Muslims respectively on a 6:5 ratio. Thus, since independence, the number of deputies in parliament has been a multiple of eleven, a total of the 6:5 ratio, and since 1960 a full parliament has consisted of 99 members (see Table 6.2).

The allocation of seats according to religious groups, a system known as confessionalism, is essentially a form of proportional representation, designed to reconcile societies which contain numerous religious communities. A similar system, in which political positions were shared on religious grounds, was in operation during the years of the French mandate and, as such, was both established and workable at the time of Lebanon's independence. It is quite possible, of course, to see the colonial experience as instrumental in forging political tradition in the Lebanon as had been the case in other colonial territories. The National Covenant was not, in fact, a formal constitution but rather an addendum to the Constitution

Table 6.1 Religious communities in Lebanon according to the 1932 census

	Number of people	*Percentage of population*
Maronite	261,043	30
Greek Orthodox	90,275	10
Greek Catholic	52,602	6
Armenian	34,296	4
Other Christians	14,065	2
All Christians	**452,281**	**52**
Sunni	182,842	21
Shi'te	158,425	18
Druze	56,812	6.5
All Muslims	**398,079**	**45.5**
Jews	10,469	1
Total	**860,829**	

Source: B. M. Borthwick, *Comprative Politics of The Middle East* (New Jersey, 1980)

Notes: *A breakdown of the Muslim and Christian Communities*

Muslim

Sunni	The mainstream school of thought in Islam.
Shi'ite	A branch of Islam which split from the Sunni over the question of succession to the Prophet Muhammad.
Druze	A secretive sect adhering to the mystical teachings of Fatimid Caliph al-Hakim (996–1021 AD), often considered as non-Muslim by many Muslims.
Alawites	A schism of Shi'ite Islam, despised by the mainstream Sunni community, an estimated 50,000 sect members live in and around Tripoli.

Christian

Maronites	A formally Aramaic speaking Christian people, native to the Syrian area, who settled in Mount Lebanon to escape persecution during the tenth century. Entered into communion in 1736 with the Roman See as a Uniate Church retaining own rites, ceremonies, canon law and bishops, but recognizing the Pope's authority.
Greek Orthodox	The Arabic speaking followers of the Eastern Church are centred in the Beka'a valley.
Greek Catholics	Also known as Melchites, a splinter group from the Greek Orthodox Church who have entered into communion with Rome as a Uniate Church.
Armenian Orthodox	The Armenians have sought refuge in Lebanon from massacres in Turkey since the 1890s. Their church, one of the oldest in Christendom, is in communion with the Greek Orthodox Church. The community is centred on Beirut and its suburbs.
Armenian Catholics	The Uniate split from their Orthodox Church.
Syrian Orthodox	An old Orthodox sect linked to the Nestorians from modern day Turkey, who fled to Lebanon having suffered extensive persecution alongside the Armenians at the hands of the Ottoman Turks.
Syrian Catholics	The Uniate split from their Orthodox Church.

Assyrian Catholics	Also known as the Nestorians, adherents of an early Christian heresy, concerning the nature of Christ.
Chaldean Catholics	The Uniate split in the Nestorian community.
Roman Catholics	In complete communion with the Pope.
Protestants	Includes Anglicans, Baptists, and Evangelical Churches from Europe and America.
Judaism	A small community still exists in Beirut.

Table 6.2 Apportionment of religious groups in the National Assembly 1972

Maronite Catholics	30
Sunni Muslims	20
Shi'a Muslims	19
Greek Orthodox	11
Greek-Melkite Catholics	6
Druzes	6
Armenian Orthodox	4
Armenian Catholics	1
Protestants	1
Minorities	1
Total	99

promulgated in 1926, by the French authorities. According to that constitution, personal freedom and freedom of the press were guaranteed and protected, religious communities were entitled to maintain their own schools, the rights of the ownership were protected by the law and every Lebanese citizen over 21 years of age was enfranchised. These provisions were carried through to independent Lebanon. The National Covenant delineated a parliamentary form of government, with legislative power exercised by one house, whose members had to be literate, over 25 years and in possession of full political and civil rights. The usual term of deputies is four years with general elections occuring within 60 days. Parliament, which can be suspended only by a two-thirds majority, holds two sessions annually: March–May and October–December, and on constitutional issues a quorum of two-thirds and a majority vote is required among deputies.

However, despite the apparent emphasis on a parliamentary mode of government the Lebanon has a strong executive presidency dominating over a tamed and docile National Assembly.[4] The president is elected by the assembly for a period of six years. He can initiate laws and in turn appoints the ministers and the prime minister. He can also dissolve the National Assembly and force an election. Of course, one of the major difficulties with the apparatus of government is that it is deficient in terms of representation. It has long been recognized that the 1932 census is profoundly misleading as to precise religious percentages and that Lebanon should have a constitution which actually gives its Muslim population an equal share of power. Another major source of discontent with the country's political structures is the belief that the 'general welfare' and 'good of the country' are not operating principles and generally each sect thinks of its own interests.[5] The lack of common loyalty and political cohesion militates against the development of a fully-fledged pluralistic society; each group is concerned with its own separate entity and has little interest in others.[6] Although this is regarded as a characteristic of Arab society generally, on occasions it is possible for alliances between different groups to be forged on a shifting basis.[7] Thus, association can be forged on immediate interests and Professor Fuad Khuri points to the example of the changing allegiances of the militias in Beirut in the early 1980s.[8]

Dominant interests

The term 'national integration' as outlined by Myron Weiner, refers to the problem of linking government with the governed. Implied within this usage is the familiar notion of a 'gap' between the elite and the masses, characterized by marked differences in aspirations and values.[9] Undoubtedly, there is a preponderance of business men and landlords among deputies of the National Assembly some of whom are connected to families who have been involved in the political life of the country for many years. Also the control exerted by political bosses, or 'za'ims', who owe their position to their financial power and political inheritance, has led to the assertion that elections in Lebanon are not in any sense free.[10] The za'ims, because of their influence and dominance in particular localities, have to be courted by any aspiring parliament candidate. Such a process inevitably leads to subservience to the za'im in the Assembly or, if the za'im happens to be a cabinet minister, complete obedience is demanded. It is, perhaps, not surprising to learn that 'twenty families have each contributed more than one cabinet minister since the establishment of the French Mandate after the First World War'.[11]

The electoral system, in which ballots are cast at the place of birth rather than of residence tends to reinforce the authority of the za'ims. The fact that the country is divided into electoral districts, each with a number of seats allocated to different religious groups which reflect their percentage size, has contributed to the development of electoral lists. The lists, therefore, contain a selection of candidates representing different religious sectors. However, all voters irrespective of their religious affiliation, are free to choose candidates for the available seats in their locality. The voters actually have to make decisions and choices about representatives of other denominational groups. This system can undermine the accusation that the confessional process panders to the electorates' narrow sectarian interests. It is within this context that the selection of candidates for the lists become increasingly important. A za'im will often not only head a list but will also choose representatives from other sects to join his list. This process leads to a degree of cooperation between the various religious groups, thus reducing potential conflict, but as Tareq Ismael warns, it can serve to further enhance the power and dominance of the za'im.[12] It is alleged that a za'im will often use his political position in a variety of different ways, for example, 'to speed up the granting of a (business) licence, get someone out of jail, or improve a road in a particular area'.[13]

Nevertheless, patronage, interest groups affinities, business sympathies and exchanged favours are not exactly unknown in other political systems. The difference is, of course, the prominent role played by political parties in other countries and their relative unimportance in Lebanon. Yet the confessional system of government has not inhibited the formation of political parties, it is only their influence which is held in check. According to reports in 1990 there exist numerous political organizations (see Table 6.3) and around 40 per cent of deputies are associated with a political grouping.[14] This figure represents an increase on the elections held in 1960, 1964 and 1968, following which studies suggest around one-third of parliamentary members represented political parties.[15]

Political parties

The Lebanese Christian parties, 'Al-Kataeb' and Phalanges Libanaises, had seven members in the National Assembly and the National Liberal Party, 'Al-Wataniyin al-Ahrar' had nine members, before the two organizations merged in 1979. With such a large array of parties there was a tendency to coalesce into political blocs as happened in 1976 with the formation of the Lebanese Front and the National Front.

The Lebanese Front comprised an assortment of right-wing parties under the direction of the Phalange, whilst the National Front represented a grouping of left-wing parties, mainly Muslim, the most important of which were the Progressive Socialist Party (PSP), led by Kemal Jumblatt, who also led the Front, and the Syrian Social National Party (PPS). The most important feature of certain political parties was neither their ideology nor their membership figures but the maintenance of trained, and armed private militias which could withstand attack. These private armies could be seen as protecting the party or alleviating civil disorder; either way the militias posed a challenge to the Lebanese army, especially when the civil war engulfed the country and during the strife-torn years which followed.

The preponderance of these numerous militias could be viewed as an illustration of the emerging 'gap' between the state and the people and they certainly contributed towards Lebanon's political disintegration. But the Lebanese experience did not correspond with the notion that such a 'gap' is exacerbated by the elite's attempts to coerce and control the masses.[16] In the case of Lebanon it was quite the opposite, the separate militias were largely autonomous organizations essentially pursuing their own interests unencumbered by a dominant state. It was this development, rather than

Table 6.3 Political organizations

Armenian Revolutionary Federation
Al-Ba'ath (Syrian wing)
Al-Ba'ath (Iraqi wing)
Bloc National
Ad-Dustur (Constitutional Party)
Al-Harakiyines Al-Arab
Al-Hayat Al-Wataniya
Al-Hizb Ad-Damuqratiya Al-Barlamaniya (Christian Social Democratic Party)
Al-Jabha Al-Damuqratiya Al-Barlamaniya (Parliamentary Democratic Front)
Al-Kata'eb (Phalangist Party)
Mouvement de L'action Nationale
An-Najjade (The Helpers)
An-Nida Al-Kawmi (National Struggle)
Parti Communiste Libanais (Lebanese Communist Party)
Parti Democrate
Parti National Liberal
Parti Socialiste Nationaliste Syrien
Parti Socialiste Progressiste
Parti Socialiste Revolutionnaire
Amal

Source: *Middle East and North Africa*, (London, 1990)

the confessional system per se, which profoundly debilitated the nation's political balance especially when external pressures became critical.

External factors

The Lebanese civil war of 1975/76 resulted in the loss of nearly 40,000 lives.[17] Pierre Gemayal, founder of the Phalangist Party, lamented the demise of Lebanon's 'happiest period': 'Between 1943 and 1970 . . . we were free and independent . . . We had a very special system in Lebanon, a parliamentary democratic system . . . with equal rights for the 17 religious communities and freedom of expression for every man and woman be they Muslim or Christian.'[18] In Gemayal's view the country's deteriorating political climate was the direct result of Palestinian activity in Lebanon following their ejection from Jordan in 1971. It was, of course, difficult for Lebanon not to be involved in the Palestinian-Israeli dispute given its proximity to Israel and the fact that the country housed Palestinian refugee camps.

The Cairo Agreements signed in November 1969 by the Commander-in-Chief of the Lebanese army and Yasser Arafat of the PLO, confined Palestinian guerrilla activity to certain areas, in order to prevent Lebanese civilian casualties. Yet this agreement did little to ease Christian fears of the Palestinians becoming 'a state within a state' as Israel stepped up its reprisal attacks against Palestinian bases in the southern flank of the country. Jordanian fears about the Palestinian impact on that country now were being echoed within Lebanon. It was a fraught period under the presidency of Suleyman Franjiya. The 1973 Arab-Israeli war foreshadowed PLO moves to establish closer alliances with Lebanese Muslim groups, thus giving greater momentum to their familiar plea for greater representation in parliament and in the allocation of government posts. These demands set in motion similar claims from other groups. The Shi'a Muslims of southern Lebanon, who would become especially prominent in future years, also called for greater representation, investment and development of their area. If the government failed to respond the Shi'a leader, Imam Musa Sadr, warned of his intention to organize and arm his followers as a protection against Israeli raids, which, of course, he later did.

The plight of Shi'ites was dire, an impoverished neglected community with very little political influence, who were feeling the full brunt of Israeli attacks. In 1974 Musa Sadr led a non-violent protest of some 100,000 Shi'ites demanding equality for the community and calling on the government to take action to stop Israeli punitive raids on southern Lebanon, which although directed against Palestinian fighters were, in actuality, killing Shi'ites and destroying their villages.[19] The Shi'ites pleas went unheeded as events overtook debate.

Although intercommunal tension had never been far from the surface an incident in April 1975 tipped the balance and the country plunged into a civil war. A prominent Phalangist was assassinated by a Palestinian and as a reprisal, 27 Palestinians were killed. The event sparked a series of clashes between Muslims and Christians. In the first phase of the conflict, leftist Lebanese Muslims, including the Druze allied with PLO groups, seized the offensive on a platform of constitutional and economic reforms in favour of the Muslim community, now widely regarded as outnumbering the Christians. These demands placed pressures on the government and in 1975 a national dialogue committee was formed consisting of 20 members from all political and confessional groups with the brief to restore 'normal life' to the country; on any reckoning, a gargantuan task.

Despite a temporary cease-fire in 1976 there was no agreement reached on political reforms and conflict flared again. The major difficulty with granting greater representation to the Muslim community was the fact that it reduced the authority of the Christian sector who were unwilling to concede any reduction of their power. It was not surprising that no agreement could be reached. Instead the president took a radical step. In April 1976, he requested the assistance of Syrian forces, which duly entered the country under the title of the 'Arab Deterrent Force' (ADF), a decision which was ratified by the Arab League. This move was tantamount to an admission of defeat and a sign that the country was becoming a virtual battleground. Indiscriminate killing became widespread as the country divided into warring zones. Although Franjiya was replaced by President Elias Sarkis and the government was granted emergency powers and permitted to rule by decree for six months, it was clear the conflict was developing into a 'war of proxy' as neighbouring powers, Syria and Israel became further embroiled and Lebanon became simply a theatre of war.

Inevitably these developments were reflected in the political arena as allegiances were formed, the Phalangist Party aligned with Israel, and Muslim groups were sympathetically disposed to the Palestinians. It was during this time that the private militias, rapidly gaining in strength and belligerency, profoundly undermined Lebanon's political structures.

Ethnic division/interests

The political divisions manifested during the war put immense strain on the sectarian apportionment of power within the confessional system. For three months in 1980 there was no functioning government although President Sarkis remained in office. In 1982 Israel launched a full-scale invasion of the country. The Phalangist commander, Bashir Gemayel announced his presidential ambitions and was assassinated. By way of reprisal the Phalangist militia entered the Palestinian refugee camps of Sabra and Chatila and killed residents. Bashir's brother Amin was elected president but although he too was a Phalangist and pro-Israeli, he had a reputation as a moderate. Yet the divisions were too great and he was without support among Shi'ites who continually opposed the Israeli invasion.

Three Shi'ite groups were operating: Amal (Hope) Movement; Hizbollah (Party of God) and the Lebanese Communist Party/Organization of Communist Action in Lebanon. The Amal movement was the largest group, founded by Musal Sadr and led by a lawyer, Nabih Berri. It called for the withdrawal of all foreign forces from the country, the unification of Lebanon, the co-existence of confessional groups and more power for the Shi'ite community. The Hizbollah party was a fundamentalist movement which had grown significantly since the Israeli invasion. The movement had also been assisted by the Revolutionary Guards sent to Lebanon from Iran. Its key leaders were Sheikh Fadlullah and Hussein Mussawi, who until 1982 had been Amal's military commander. The aim of Hizbollah was to turn Lebanon into an Islamic republic. The underground Islamic Jihad, had suspected affiliations to Hizbollah. The Lebanese Communist Party and Organization of Communist Action in Lebanon although small and ideologically separate, joined forces with the PLO in Lebanon. The Shi'ites began their overt military and political campaign in 1983 with attacks on the United States and European Multinational Force in Beirut and the blowing up of the US embassy. By 1984 the Shi'ites led by Amal in association with Hizbollah, rose in Beirut against the Lebanese army and took control of the Western sector.

Reports at the time described the situation in Beirut as bleak, reminiscent of the civil war with: 'a divided capital city, a helpless or non-existent army, a beleagured President with little real authority and with his opponents calling for his removal'.[20] In short, it appeared that Lebanon's state structure might completely disintegrate. It had been the Amal leader, Nabih Berri's calls for the resignation of Muslim cabinet ministers which precipitated the resignation of the government. With Beirut divided along the so-called 'Green Line', into Christian and Muslim-controlled districts, prognoses in the Arab press were dispiriting. Lebanon in the future would never be more than 'a sort of sectarian coalition or factional alliance which will never be permitted, nor able, to reconstitute a united state or people'.[21] Others viewed the success of the Shi'ite militiamen of the Amal movement as bringing dangerously close the possibility of the establishment of an Islamic republic on part of Lebanon's territory. Although Berri was a moderate in the Islamic camp, it was felt that Ayatollah Khomeini had designs on Lebanon and had managed to influence a significant section of the Shi'ite community.[22] The Shi'ites had, of course, been the country's most deprived community and were responsive to calls for action. It seemed that any negotiations about Lebanon's future would be predicated on a deal between Christian and Shi'ites, with the Sunni Druze and other communities taking a back seat. However, one basic problem existed: what kind of a polity should Lebanon be? Was it to be a relatively strong, centralized state with power shared equally between Christians and Muslims? Or should it be a loose federation of confessional entities ceding only marginal powers to Beirut? Was it, indeed, possible to unify the state at this time, and most crucially, what was Lebanon's relationship to be with Israel, Syria and Iran.

The search for unity

In March 1984, as a result of Syrian pressure, President Gemayal abrogated an agreement he had concluded with Israel mediated through the United States, for the removal of all foreign troops from the country, in return for Syrian guarantees of internal security. Shortly after a government of national unity was appointed under the Sunni Muslim, Rashid Karami. For a brief period it was hoped the Karami government could initiate a move towards uniting the country but it was not long before hopes foundered on factional confrontation. Whilst Israel declared that 'peace would not come to south Lebanon', reports revealed the parlous nature of the situation: 'It was a full month before parliament could be called into session and give the vote of confidence necessary for the government to assume full constitutional powers. The speaker, Kamel al-Assad, refused to convene it until special security arrangements had been agreed. Within an hour of the announcement of the parliamentary date, gunmen had kidnapped a group of innocent victims'.[23] Karami, himself was to be assassinated in June 1987.

Although Israeli forces withdrew from Lebanon in mid-1985 they remained in effective control of the border area, and alert to the presence of

Syrian troops and the resumed presence of the PLO. However, during the second half of the 1980s, the Christian-Muslim divide deteriorated as vicious conflicts flared between rival factions within, rather than between, the two camps. It seemed that events were spiralling out of control with all factions locked into struggles they were unlikely to win. The traditional antagonism between the Sunni and Shi'a Muslims was exacerbated as the Amal movement attacked a Sunni trade union organization, the Union of the Forces of Working People in 1985. This action led directly to calls for a general strike which immobilized the country. The political crisis which foreshadowed the assassination of Karami included a combination of factors: a large increase in the price of basic commodities and a concomitant rise in poverty; the absence of any solution to the country's sectarian conflict, and the resultant wave of strikes and demonstrations by all religious groups, protesting at the decline of living standards. The Lebanese press reported the country's yearning to return to normal life and 'to bridle the power of the parties and organisations if they seek to perpetuate the present situation'.[24] Yet given the nature of the conflict and the number of states involved and affecting domestic Lebanese politics it is difficult to imagine how this could have been achieved. As the Amal movement began to engage in fighting against the PLO and the Hizbollah it was almost as though a free-for-all contest of strength was being waged on Lebanese territory.

Political disintegration

President Gemayal's term of office was due to expire in 1988 and the National Assembly was required to elect a new president. Inevitably, the prospect aroused some apprehension. The elections of previous presidents had produced extraordinary scenes: the shelling of parliament as deputies arrived to vote in 1976 and the frogmarching into the chamber of the last members needed for a quorum, with Israeli troops stationed outside, in 1982.

The 1988 attempts to elect a president were set to produce a constitutional crisis and further divided the country. As the election neared, political manoeuvrings began in order to find a candidate who should be a Maronite Christian but would also be acceptable to both Christians and Muslims. The difficulty with this quest rested in the divisions within the Maronite community together with the resistance of most Christians to accepting a candidate who was suspected of representing the interests of Syria. The Syrians favoured the candidacy of former president, Suleyman Franjiya, but the National Assembly failed to produce a quorum at the necessary electoral sessions. On one of those occasions only 14 deputies actually arrived at the parliamentary building in West Beirut to cast their votes; other Christian deputies assembled in a building in East Beirut and repeated their opposition to Franjiya.[25] Ultimately, and only a matter of minutes before his term of office expired, President Gemayal appointed a six-member interim military government, composed of three Christian and three Muslim officers, led by the Maronite Commander-in-Chief of Armed Forces, General Michel Aoun. However, the Muslim nominees refused to serve under General Aoun and declared their support for the Syrian-backed caretaker government of Selim al-Hoss, who had been acting Prime Minister since 1987.

Thus, by the end of September 1988, Lebanon had no president and two governments both of which claimed legitimacy: one Christian, under General Aoun in east Beirut, the other, predominantly Muslim, under Selim al-Hoss in west Beirut. It seemed that all the talk of partition had finally crystallized into reality with the country now manifestly divided into two competing governments. In a sense, the result was a distorted outcome of Lebanon's form of democracy. Within a system in which the president is elected by deputies in the National Assembly, rather than by universal suffrage it would only be a matter of time before deputies succumbed to external pressures with ultimately divisive consequences. As for the will of the people, it is generally assumed their opinions went either unnoticed or ignored. The Beirut newspaper, 'As-Safir' warned that the political situation was not in the interests of the Lebanese people regardless of 'individual sect, group, faith or political faction'.[26] It is important to remember that the Lebanon possessed a politically aware, educated population, 83 per cent of whom lived in urban areas with wide access to the media. Of a population of three million, two million had radios and 800,000 televisions. In fact, the media station Tele-Liban was a multi-channel commercial service.[27] Yet with political life virtually suspended for the average citizen their power to influence matters was limited. In any case once the militias had taken hold there existed every chance of being gunned down in a wave of indiscriminate shootings. It was only a matter of months before General Aoun declared his 'war of liberation' against Syria, thereby, initiating another dimension to the country's conflict and sparking off some of the bloodiest fighting witnessed in Beirut during the previous 14 years. The death toll in the six months between March and September 1989 was estimated to be around 1000 which resulted in the intervention of yet another external force, the Arab League, who produced an accord for national reconciliation.

It is perhaps appropriate that the Arab League should intervene. If political disintegration came to Lebanon at the hands of regional pressures, then so too should political rehabilitation. However, for such a process to occur, the Lebanese deputies had to meet outside the country and as such, in 1980 a meeting took place in Taif, Saudi Arabia. The majority of deputies agreed to an 'accord' and under its terms, they elected a new president, Rene Mouawad. But it was not to be so straightforward, the 'accord' was rejected by General Aoun on the grounds that it did not provide for the immediate withdrawal of Syrian troops and the new President-elect was assassinated. However, time was running out for General Aoun and when yet another president, the Maronite Christian, President Hirawi, formed a new government led by Dr al-Hoss and including Nabih Berri of the Amal movement and Druze leader Walid Jumblatt a government of national reconciliation won a unanimous vote of confidence from the deputies. Although Aoun complained that the election had been 'illegal and unconstitutional', he was formally dismissed from his post as army commander in 1989 and finally expelled from his stronghold in east Beirut the following year.

Political reform

In September 1990 President Hirawi signed a series of constitutional amendments which codified a number of political reforms. These amendments stemmed directly from the 'accords' reached at the deputies' meeting in Taif, and later endorsed in Beirut. The features of the new constitution were quite radical. The National Assembly was to be expanded from 99 to 108 members, and to be equally divided between Christians and Muslims, thereby abolishing the old 6:5 ratio; the post of prime minister and the role of the cabinet was to be upgraded whilst the position and powers of the presidency were to be correspondingly reduced. The reforms clearly represented moves towards a more democratic and equitable political system. Of the nine new seats for Muslims, three would be allocated for Shi'as and two each for the Sunni, Alawi and Druze communities.

Through the defeat of Aoun it was possible to dismantle the 'Green Line', which effectively separated Muslim west and Christian east Beirut and permitted the establishment of a security plan intended to begin a process of disarming the militias in and around the areas. The Lebanese Front, the PSP and the Amal issued immediate statements declaring their intentions to withdraw from Beirut and to hand over positions to the Lebanese Army. Yet almost as a reminder of the awfulness of the recent strife, Dany Chamoun, president of the right-wing National Liberal Party and a prominent supporter of Aoun, was assassinated in east Beirut in October 1990. He was the son of the former Lebanese President Camille Chamoun and one of the remaining hereditary leaders in the country. The killing raised questions about the government's ability to quench sporadic acts of violence and about its precise relationship with Syria. Along with its programme of reform, the Taif Agreement had recognized Syria's special 'fraternal' relations with Lebanon. The agreement stipulated that the Syrian army should withdraw from Beirut and its hinterland within two years of the establishment of a new government, but it did not set a date for Syrian forces to leave Lebanon as a whole. Also when a new government was formed under Umar Karami, brother of the former Prime Minister, disquiet was expressed among Phalangists at the appointment of pro-Syrians to the key posts of Minister of National Defence and Minister of the Interior. Some commentators suggested that General Aoun had been right all along in his condemnation of the Taif Agreement, in that it placed Lebanon's independence from Syria, 'in jeopardy'.

Treaty with Syria

There is no doubt that the Treaty signed between Syria and Lebanon on 22 May 1991 was far-reaching. The Treaty of Brotherhood, strived to achieve cooperation and coordination between the two countries, in the field of politics, economics, security, science and culture. Article Three contained the treaty's key clause:

> The connection between the security of the two countries requires that Lebanon must not become a source of threat to Syria's security and vice versa under any circumstance. Therefore, Lebanon will not allow itself to become a transit point or base for any force, state or organisation that seeks to undermine its security or that of Syria.[28]

The statement was a clear reference to the involvement of Israel, Iran and the PLO in the affairs of Lebanon which were viewed as, not only, destabilizing influences within the country, but also, forces which threatened Syria's security. As such, Article Four stipulated that in line with the provisions of the Taif Agreement, Syrian forces would be redeployed subject to joint Lebanese-Syrian military specifications. The administrative structure facilitating the objectives of the treaty were outlined in Article Six. The Supreme Council, consisting of the presidents of both countries, would meet at least once a year to chart the general policy for coordination and cooperation and its decisions would be 'binding and effective within the framework of the constitutional laws and rules of Syria and Lebanon'. The Executive Committee, on which the two premiers sit, would meet at least once every six months in order to coordinate the implementation of the Supreme Council's decisions. Additionally, three specialized committees were established: Foreign Affairs; Economic and Social Affairs; and Defence and Security Affairs, all of which would meet every two months.

Whilst some commentators argue that the treaty is nothing more than the virtual annexation of Lebanon by Syria, Article Three does raise the question of Lebanon's independence: 'Syria, which cherishes Lebanon's security, independence and unity and the agreement among its people, will not allow any action that threatens Lebanon's security, independence and sovereignty.'[29] The Lebanese President, Ilyas al-Hirawi speaking in May 1991 attempted to reassure the population by claiming that the country was: 'Too impregnable to be assimilated and too lofty to be changed.'[30] Nevertheless, the treaty has been condemned as a 'treaty of submission', imposed on a weak and paralysed Lebanon, undermining the country's freedom and sovereignty and abolishing its independence.[31] The ex-president Amin Gemayal, pointed to the fact that Lebanon had always advocated democratic and liberal values: 'For decades we experimented with the democratic and parliamentary system and exercised it to the full within an open and liberal democracy. Now this very democracy is being delivered into the hands of Syrian dictatorship.'[32]

It is, perhaps, inevitable that such an alliance between Lebanon and Syria should arouse some contention. The 16 years of civil war which divided Lebanon into warring zones had an especially deleterious impact on its political system. In 1988 Lebanon was without a President, had two rival half-governments, and a process of partition seemed almost inevitable. The situation, unprecedented since the country attained independence in 1943, seemed to defy solution until, that is, the Gulf crisis of 1990/91 shifted allegiances in the Middle East. With Syria's decision to move towards the West, peace in Lebanon has been seen as a 'marvellous, unlooked-for bonus from the Gulf War', and if Syria were closely involved in the procedure, 'then so be it'.[33] However, there are real and distinctly different styles of government and political life in Lebanon and contemporary Syria.

Post-Gulf War 1991

There is no doubt that the years of war have exacted a price and Syrian involvement may be seen as necessary during the transition to peace.[34] Possibly, the constitutional reforms offer a tangible indication of a more stable political system and a return to democratic life. Certainly, the general election which took place in the summer of 1992, was the first for twenty years. Although, according to local officials, the election aroused strong feelings and was far from perfectly organized, their opinions were unanimous: 'Elections are better than fighting.'[35]

Lebanon's confessional electoral system may actually help to preserve democracy especially now that Islamic organizations participate in democratic exercises. As the Shi'a community is the country's largest religious group it is claimed that it could command significant electoral support. However, within the Lebanese parliament, operating on a system of proportional representation Shi'a candidates would be capable of winning only a fixed percentage of seats. With fears surrounding the possible ulterior motives and ambitions of Islamic parties and their true commitment to democracy, it might be that confessionalism offers a process of controlled democratic participation which would help preserve stability. Also, if Syria were to consider reform, a consociational model of political interaction might be an appropriate starting point.

Conclusion

At first sight it would seem that the political disintegration Lebanon suffered during the years of war and conflict reflected a profound inadequacy of the nation's political system. Yet the vulnerability of Lebanon's political structures may not only be due to the inadequacies of the confessional model of government, the past inexactitude of the 6:5 religious divide or the fact that political leaders served particular interests, although of course these factors all played a part; rather, external dynamics in the form of the Palestinian presence, the resultant Israeli attack and penetration and the involvement of Syria combined to undermine and split the country. In addition, the Islamic revolution in Iran aroused and encouraged the Shi'a community in Lebanon who were caught up in the Israeli/Palestinian conflagration. Political disintegration, then, can occur as a result of external actions. Regional pressures in the form of unresolved conflicts, the military preparedness of neighbouring states and the impact of religious revival shaped and distorted Lebanon's political structures. In short, the political system of Lebanon was as much affected by regional dispute and contention as the political development of other states in the area had been damaged by Cold War rivalry and interference. If Cold War competitiveness is no longer a political dynamic in the Middle East, it must be hoped that regional influences will be conducive to political reform.

It is as well to remember that Jordan suffered a civil war because of external penetration resulting from the unresolved Arab/Israeli conflict. In a sense, it is surprising that those countries facing the full impact of that conflict survive at all. Inevitably, existing societal polarizations will be exacerbated especially if they are finely tuned and potentially volatile. Lebanon did manage to sustain a form of democracy, a relatively open press, a formal method of political participation and a degree of political discourse during a period which witnessed revolutions, coups and counter-coups occurring within the region as a whole. Whatever the deficiencies of the confessional model it did manage to function at governmental level and established a tradition of political behaviour of which the Lebanese people were proud. It is ironic that elections should return to a war-ravaged nation at the behest and under the tutelage of a dominant party state, Syria. But return they have and that must be regarded as a move in a more positive direction. The extent of Lebanon's independence is too early to quantify but it would seem that certain features of democracy may be upheld.

Prospects for democracy

The politics of the Third World has excited considerable attention over the years. Some studies have examined the literature and the various schools of analysis; others have provided an overview of political approaches in various regions and in particular countries, and others, still, have sought to identify clear linkages between very different nations and so establish a theoretical definition to political processes in the Third World.[1] This chapter places the Middle East within the larger debate about the prospects for democracy in the Third World, in order to discover whether or not the region is distinctive in some systematic and significant way. Or the extent to which the area shares commonalities in the political, historical and economic spheres with other countries of the Third World.

Cammack, Poole and Tordoff, in their comparative study of the Middle East, Africa and Latin America, maintain that

> Under the aegis of a broadly comparable process, differences in timing, intensity and mechanisms of Western capitalist expansion (and differences in the nature and response of existing indigenous societies, political systems and cultures) provide a framework for understanding the contrasting political experience of the Third World.[2]

Such a framework, they suggest, permits variations between regions and between states within regions to be explained 'as a function of different levels of economic and political penetration and interaction with widely different constellations of local factors'.[3] It would be appropriate, then, in considering issues raised in earlier chapters, to start with the role of external control and influence, and then to move on to other areas: citizenship and national integration; Islam and socio-economic factors, before finally examining the prospects for democracy in the Middle East.

Table 7.1

Country	*Colonial experience*
Syria	Independence 1946. French control, Mandated 1920–46 Under control of Ottoman Empire (Turkish) 1516–1918 Seventh century AD Syria centre of Arab empire.
Lebanon	Full independence 1944. French control mandate 1920–44; 1926 semi-autonomous republic with French drafted constitution. Under Ottoman Empire rule 1516–1918
Iraq	Independence 1932. British control mandate 1920–32 Under control of Ottoman Empire 1534–1918. Occupied by Britain during the Second World War because of German sympathies
Iran	No formal colonial control but interference from Britain, Germany and USSR. Former Persian empire. Changed name from Persia to Iran (meaning Aryan) in 1935
Jordan	Full independence 1946. Semi-independent in 1928. British Mandate. Autonomous status since 1923. Under control of Ottoman Empire 1517–1918
Kuwait	Full independence 1961. Al-Sabah rule from eighteenth century. Protectorate status under Britain since 1899 in order to prevent Ottoman interference. Iraq has claimed sovereignty over Kuwait on the grounds that it was part of the Basra province in Ottoman times
Israel	New state formed 1948 from the partition of Palestine recommended by United Nations Resolution 181. Palestine was under British mandate from 1922–48. The Palestinian Arabs did not accept partition

External control/influence

According to Christopher Clapham, European colonial rule had a major global impact in that 'it created political territories which were artificial, in the sense that they did not arise from the societies which they governed but were instead imposed on them'.[4] Cammack et al. see exposure to European colonial rule as the lynchpin uniting different Third World regions: 'It is clear that Africa and the Middle East share certain social and political problems resultant from the imposition of colonial boundaries on multi-communal and regionally differentiated societies.'[5]

As Table 7.1 indicates the 26 years of direct European colonial rule in all the countries contained in this study, with the exception of Iran, succeeded four-hundred years of domination by the Turkish (Ottoman) Empire. One analyst points to the bureaucratic nature of the Ottoman Empire with the 'concentration of political power in the hands of the Sultan and his military and civilian bureaucrats' as an explanation for the absence of representative institutions'.[6] There is no doubt that when the Ottoman Empire collapsed during the First World War, the Middle East witnessed a 'carve-up of

Ottoman spoils by the Allied powers which was a cynical act of self-interest'.[7] One of the major condemnations of the San Remo conference in 1920, the occasion when the apportionment of territories was arranged, was the fact that in the construction of artificial nation-state delineations, nationalities were left 'straddling borders'. The Kurds, for instance, were 'divided between Iraq, Iran and Turkey'.[8] The Kurds, of course, had been divided roughly on a ratio of 75:25 between the Ottoman Empire and Persia (Iran) since the sixteenth century, but the impact of European colonization left them in enclaves within nation-states. The territorial impact of European colonialism cannot be over-stated but this is not to argue that the Ottoman Empire, based on a system of tribute, carried no territorial implications. The rationale of Iraq's claims to Kuwait is based on the grounds that it formed part of a regional appropriation under the aegis of the Ottoman Empire, not because of some former suzerainty in a pre-Ottoman era.[9]

The short period of European control resulted in certain landowning and merchant families continuing an ascendancy which developed during the latter years of the Ottoman Empire. The French mandates for Syria and Lebanon followed a divide-and-rule policy which eventually emerged into a form of confessionalism in Lebanon and a split nationalist movement, nevertheless, much opposition in Syria. It was the 1932 census conducted during the French mandatory period which was the basis of the 6:5 Christian/Muslim ratio that was in operation in Lebanon until 1991. The Lebanese Constitution promulgated in 1926 by the French authorities formed the basis of the National Covenant which Lebanon introduced in 1943, and which has remained in operation.

The most contentious aspect of Britain's period of colonial rule was the 'dual obligation' contained in the Mandate for Palestine, i.e. the commitment to independence and self-government for the Palestinian Arabs together with the promise of establishing a Jewish national homeland. The conflicting nature of these two commitments created fear, distrust and a groundswell of anti-Western sentiment, the implications of which are discussed later in the chapter.

The literature of the 1950s and 1960s refers to the emergence of 'new' states. Iran, whose history dates back as far as the sixth century BC, who controlled an Empire which extended to the eastern Mediterranean, and who actually was under no formal colonial control, was grudgingly described by one academic in his eagerness to define and describe the 'new' nations as 'not a new state in the strict sense, perhaps'.[10] The grouping of the states in the Middle East as somehow 'new' denies their dynamic history and, indeed, in the pre-Ottoman period their own capacity for conquest and territorial control. What is witnessed after the Second World War is a process which was half-forged in the inter-war period, that is, an attempted shift away from British and French colonial rule. Independence, however, was to be marred by another period of external interference, that of the United States and the Soviet Union under the guise of the Cold War.

Table 7.2 Social and economic data for the eastern Mediterranean and the Gulf states

EASTERN MEDITERRANEAN: Social and economic data

	GNP per capita (US$)		*Life expectancy (yrs)*			*Adult literacy (% of pop)*		*Population with access to safe water (%)*	*Under-five mortality rate (per 1000)*		*Daily calorie supply (as % of requirements)*	
	1976	*1987*	*1960*	*1975*	*1987*	*1970*	*1985*	*1985–7*	*1960*	*1988*	*1964–6*	*1984–6*
Israel	3920	6800	69	72	76	88	95	—	40	14	109	118
Jordan	610	1560	47	59	67	47	75	96	218	57	93	121
Lebanon	—	—	60	65	68	69	78	93	92	51	99	125
Syria	780	1640	50	59	66	40	60	76	218	64	89	131

	GDP ($bn)	*GNP ($bn)*	*Expenditure as % of GNP*						*Debt service (% exports)*	*Annual inflation (%)*	*Urban pop (%)*	*Breakdown of labour force (%)*					
			Health		*Education*		*Military*					*Agriculture*		*Industry*		*Services*	
	1987	*1987*	*1960*	*1986*	*1960*	*1986*	*1960*	*1986*	*1987*	*1980–87*	*1988*	*1965*	*1985–87*	*1965*	*1985–87*	*1965*	*1985–87*
Israel	35.0	29.8	1.0	2.1	8.0	7.3	2.9	19.2	25	159.0	91	12	4.9	35	22.8	53	72.3
Jordan	4.3	4.4	0.6	1.9	3.0	5.1	16.7	13.8	22	2.8	67	37	10.2	26	25.6	37	64.2
Lebanon	—	—	—	—	—	—	—	—	—	—	82	29	14.3	24	27.4	47	58.4
Syria	24.0	20.4	0.4	0.8	2.0	5.7	7.9	14.7	17	11.0	51	52	24.9	20	16.0	28	59.1

GULF STATES: Social and economic data

	GNP per capita (US$)		Life expectancy (yrs)			Adult literacy (% of pop)		Population with access to safe water (%)	Under-five mortality rate (per 1000)		Daily calorie supply (as % of requirements)	
	1976	*1987*	*1960*	*1975*	*1987*	*1970*	*1985*	*1985–7*	*1960*	*1988*	*1964–6*	*1984–6*
Bahrain	—	8510	—	—	71	—	72	100	—	—	—	—
Iran	1930	—	50	57	66	29	51	76	254	90	87	138
Iraq	1390	3020	48	59	65	34	89	87	222	94	89	124
Kuwait	15480	14610	60	68	73	54	70	—	128	22	—	—

	GDP ($bn)	GNP ($bn)	Expenditure as % of GNP: Health		Education		Military		Debt service (% exports)	Annual inflation (%)	Urban pop (%)	Breakdown of labour force (%): Agriculture		Industry		Services	
	1987	*1987*	*1960*	*1986*	*1960*	*1986*	*1960*	*1986*	*1987*	*1980–87*	*1988*	*1965*	*1985–87*	*1965*	*1985–87*	*1965*	*1985–87*
Iran	—	—	0.8	1.8	2.4	3.5	4.5	20.0	—	—	54	49	36.4	26	32.8	25	30.8
Iraq	—	—	1.0	0.8	5.8	3.7	8.7	32.0	—	—	73	50	30.4	20	22.1	30	47.5
Kuwait	17.9	27.3	—	2.9	—	4.6	—	5.8	—	4.6	95	2	1.9	34	8.7	64	89.4

Source: Keesings Record of World Events, February 1991

A brand of political thinking developed in the Middle East: pan-Arabism under Nasser or the Ba'ath Party; Arab socialism; nationalism and eventually, it might be argued, Islamic fundamentalism, all of which struck particular sentiments: anti-Western in pronouncements, radical, statist, independent. The Middle Eastern states, then, were not 'new' nations as such, but rather nations exposed to new political imperatives, e.g. the growing importance of oil and the quest to control this strategic asset; monarchies, dynasties and political leaders of long-standing contrasted with strong communist parties and the major factor of the United Nations Resolution 181, passed in November 1947, recommending the partition of Palestine into Arab and Jewish states.

Certainly, the nature of the transfer of power, that is, partition, was a policy shared by other Third World countries, and of course, India and Pakistan come to mind, both nations with very different political patterns. In a broad sense, the common experience of colonial rule does unite different nations and regions; it is after all part of their historical development. Yet the post-colonial years are important too. In the context of the Middle East and Latin America the international agenda of the Cold War was crucial, as the United States turned its attention to 'developing an anti-communist ideology' through the covert activities of the Central Intelligence Agency. As the Cold War was played out by proxy in the Middle East, covert action could be defended on the grounds of preventing the 'triumph of communism'.[11] CIA engineered coups and military pacts with the Soviet Union were not the best ways of developing a country's political structure and participatory processes, and often 'brought decades of undemocratic rule'.[12]

Numerous countries within the Middle East have been under external domination, control, exploitation and interference by empires and superpowers for consecutive periods over the past 500 years. It might not be unreasonable to deduce that these varied political and economic intrusions into their societies may be reflected in their modes and methods of political exchange and debate. Undoubtedly, there has been a strong sense of historical grievance at past, and often colonial injustices, one of the most important of which has been the Arab/Israeli dispute.

Citizenship/national integration

The partition of Palestine in 1948, a decision with which the Palestinian Arabs did not agree, has given rise to a constant source of conflict in the region. In 1960, one academic referred to the creation of the state of Israel as 'an accidental consequence' of the twentieth-century Western impact on the Middle East, which had become 'a dynamic ingredient in the Arab domestic political scene'.[13] One especially deleterious factor associated with the conflict has been the level of population displacement. There are, at present, more than 2.4 million Palestinian refugees registered with the United Nations Relief and Works Agency (UNRWA) with an annual population increase of 3 per cent. A third of that figure live in 61 camps set up by the Agency in its five fields of operation in Jordan, the West Bank, Gaza, the Lebanon and Syria. 930,000 refugees reside in Jordan, 302,000 live in Lebanon and 281,000 in Syria.[14] Whichever way the Arab/Israeli dispute is considered, the creation of Israel in 1948; the associated migration of the Palestinian population; the establishment of refugee camps; the war of 1967 and Israeli occupation of the West Bank and Gaza, are developments of enormous importance. The political implications of population mobility, displacement, subjugation and statelessness and the unresolved Palestinian question, are central concerns in the Middle East today. The most important factor in enforced demographic movement is its capacity to affect non-democracies; democratizing states and democratic states in various destabilizing ways. In short, population displacement and mobility can prevent a country from democratizing or, as in the case of Israel, may serve to undermine an ostensibly democratic state.[15] This situation has not gone unnoticed among political leaders in the Middle East. The former leader of the Israeli Labour Party warned of the damage inflicted on a country's democratic structure, by the occupation of land and people, and the Emir of Kuwait announced in March 1992 that citizenship had become the most important issue for the future.[16]

The question of citizenship, then, is strongly connected with a nation's ability to integrate its populace. National integration is specifically concerned with the problem of creating a 'sense of territorial nationality which overshadows or eliminates subordinate parochial loyalties'.[17] Accordingly, 'citizenship in a truly modern state has more and more become the most broadly negotiable claim to personal significance'. Without such an entity 'primordial loyalties will re-emerge taking the form of powerful attachments between peoples either within or outside state boundaries and centring around certain factors: blood ties, race, language, region, religion and custom'.[18] More recently, the civil and political rights associated with citizenship have been judged to be inadequate in sustaining a country's bid for democratization and, therefore, should be balanced with socio-economic rights.[19]

Certainly, the threat of national disintegration has been a continuing menace to a number of states in the region. The territorial factor has been an issue in Jordan, Israel, Lebanon, Iraq and Kuwait. The possibility of countries actually breaking-up, for example, Iraq and Lebanon, has been feared. The case studies reveal the tremendous vulnerability of the polities within the Middle East to external political developments, cf. Jordan with Palestinians, Kuwait with Iraq, Lebanon with Palestinians, Israel and Syria, which might at first sight be attributed to the claims of 'primordial loyalties'. Such susceptibility might also provide empirical evidence for Huntington's concept of the lack of 'political autonomy'. As Huntington defined it, political autonomy implied the development of political organizations and procedures which were not simply expressions of the interests of particular social groups: 'A political organization which is the instrument of a social group – family, clan, class – lacks autonomy and institutionalisation.'[20] Political organizations which were not autonomous were vulnerable to internal pressures, but more particularly to 'influences from outside the society'. Thus, 'a coup d'etat in one political system could easily 'trigger a coup d'état by similar groups in other less-developed political systems'.[21]

The political experience and, at times, instability of the states within the Middle East seem to bear out Huntington's theory. Examples exist in many states, Kuwait, Syria, Jordan, Iraq and the Lebanon, of the political dominance of certain families and clans. There are also examples of 'primordial loyalties', for instance in the case of the Kurdish peoples in Iran and Iraq whose political aspirations have been viewed as a threat to those nation-states. Yet, on another level those features of 'primordial loyalties', e.g. race, language, religion, etc. are characteristics of the region and may be regarded to be the essential nature of 'Arabness', which has both distinguished and defined certain political forms, e.g. pan-Arabism, pan-Islam. In this sense, it has been argued that any push for democracy in the area must be viewed on a regional basis as a whole rather than in individual nation-states.[22]

However, the importance of the territorial dimension of statehood within the region should not be underestimated simply on the basis of peoples sharing commonalities. The quest for a territorially defined nation statehood by the Palestinians is a strong and mobilizing force. It also poses problems if an eventual Palestinian state squeezed into the small and disjointed areas of the West Bank and Gaza proves inadequate in the absorption of Palestinian peoples living in the diaspora. The challenge to the region may be that at some stage Palestinians and 'host' countries will need to come to an agreement regarding citizenship. Host countries may have to accept and include within their citizenry Palestinians living in refugee camps or engaged in employment over a long period. Palestinians, on the other hand, who choose for one reason or another, not to live in a Palestinian state, may have to accept and remain loyal to host state nationality and citizenship. It is important to remember that whatever the affinities between the peoples in the region the interference in the politics of neighbouring states were often not casual acts of meddling or copy-cat coups d'état, although they have occurred, but were related to the Palestinians' stateless position and the associated population mobility.

So, to return to Huntington's theory. Yes, there is a lack of political autonomy within states in the region, but those polities are exacerbated by the ebbs and flows of stateless peoples. Arguably, any country in which the indigenous population is in a minority as a result of an influx of peoples would tend towards instability and a lack of autonomy. It would, therefore, be misleading to simplify or minimize the especially difficult problems population mobility and citizenship pose for the political processes of states in the region.

Islam

Islam is a major force within the spectrum of political advancement in the Middle East and elsewhere in the Third World. In recent years a debate has developed over the role played by Islamic organizations and the extent to which Islam is compatible with pluralist democracy. This discussion is centred on the functions and focus of a theocratic state. One strand of Islamic thought associates democracy with secularism, with the consequence that democracy becomes a deliberate violation of God's law and 'usurps God's role'. Democracy is seen as a foolish, absurd notion in that there can only be one relationship: that between God and man.[23] Islam, it is argued, has a totality of view, exclusive of other beliefs, which militate against full participation in multi-party politics. According to Professor Al-Azmah Islamic political groups reject the idea that they are political parties.[24]

Yet Islamic organizations do contest elections; do perform political functions and do have political programmes committed to freedom and pluralism. Clearly, then, there seem to exist contradictions within Islam which must be addressed within the context of whether or not there is an Islamic agenda for democracy. King Faud of Saudi Arabia announced that Islam was a social, political and economic system with an Islamic law providing a comprehensive constitution, comprising social justice, economic justice and the judiciary; the existence of the Qu'ran, therefore, precluded the need for a separate constitution.[25] However, the Islamic Republic of Iran relies less on the Qu'ran and more on the principles it has enshrined within its constitution, the articles of which support voter participation within the framework of an Islamic state. The best known of the 'political prescriptions' contained in the Qu'ran is that the Muslim community, the 'Umma', should have recourse to 'Shura', or consultation. In large states, 'Shura' would take place in a form of a national assembly (Majlis al-Shura).

However, in contrast to the claim that the election system is not mentioned within the legal code of 'Shari'a', Espositio and Piscatori point to the Muslim Brotherhood's decision to contest elections as far back as 1941.[26] Also in the Iranian elections to the Majlis in April 1992, over 2000 candidates, including 56 female candidates stood for 270 seats which presented voters with a multiplicity of candidates without apparent identifying labels.[27] President Rafsanjani viewed the election as important on the grounds that it enabled the government to become 'acquainted with public opinion'.[28] If participation is important in the Shi'a Islamic state of Iran, so too, at the time of Ayatollah Khomeini's rise to power, was the use of the referendum. Clearly, then, certain political features identified as 'democratic' have been, and indeed, still are, employed in Islamic states.

Modern nations are obliged to perform specific functions, economic, foreign, defence policy-making and so on. According to one specialist the two main factions of the Iranian establishment are still 'locked in fierce debates on the legality or religious merits of land distribution and other economic matters'. Choueiri goes on, 'whereas culture and politics resonate with Islamic overtones, the economy lurches in an open-ended void'.[29] The question which must be posed, then, is to what extent a modern state can actually be completely desecularized? Given the interconnectedness of the contemporary world with global trade deals and oil being sold on international markets, religious imperatives may become of secondary importance. When Rafsanjani speaks of 'pragmatism' is he really referring to Iran's adoption of 'secular' policies, and has Islam's appropriation of nationalism imposed a form of secularity upon the religion? In Professor Al-Azmah's view: 'The Arab state can be the only bulwark against Islamic totality.'[30] Whilst, according to Daniel Brumberg, 'Many in the Arab world are now wondering how the Islamic movement – and in particular the radical fundamentalists – can articulate a practical vision which effectively links Islamic values to the trying tasks of political and economic reform.'[31] Choueiri claims that 'prior to 1970, Islamic radicalism was more of an intellectual current than a political movement' and certainly a discussion has recently taken place within Islamic organizations and societies regarding changing policy.[32]

In January 1992, Sheikh Fadlallah, spiritual guide to Lebanon's Shi'ite community announced:

> A turning point has been reached in political practice. Certain currents used to call for revolution as the shortest path to power. Now the tendency among Islamic movements in the world is to take advantage of all democratic means available, which will mean participation in elections and politics.[33]

Paradoxically, it is precisely this shift in policy which has kindled fears that Islamic groups are not truly committed to a pluralist structure and democratic government. In short, the apprehension exists that Islamic parties might play the so-called 'Fascist card', playing democratic politics only to gain power, then to subsequently undermine it. Thereby, denying the basic principle in multi-party competitions for power, that is, the party which is voted into power will, in due course and through the same procedural arrangements, be voted out of office. Liberal democratic government is not only dependent on participation but also on a 'competitive struggle for the people's vote'.[34]

Yet these principles seem to have been recognized by the Iraqi oppositionist Shi'a organizations, the Supreme Assembly of the Islamic Revolution in Iraq (SAIRI) who recently outlined their new programme:

1 respect for Islamic doctrine, law and education;
2 respect for ideological freedom, political pluralism and popular opinion;
3 insistence on the unity of Iraqi territory and political unity;
4 respect for national and social pluralism;

5 commitment to the new internation trend to set up systems based on human freedom.[35]

A senior official in the US State Department, Edward Djerejian, acknowledged that the United States had been in contact with the Iraqi opposition before SAIRI issued the programme in February 1992, and according to one academic: 'The readiness of Shi'ite fundamentalist movements to form a united front with non-Islamic organizations and to adopt the principle of liberal democracy is largely the result of the invasion of Kuwait.'[36] Why Islamic groups in the post-Cold War, post-Gulf War international environment may feel the necessity to mouth liberal democratic sentiments, is unclear. Certainly, SAIRI's publication in Arabic contain ambivalent messages: 'Rather than suggestions of a liberal democratic future' statements assert 'a clear commitment to the establishment of Islamic rule in a liberated Iraq, without any qualifications'.[37]

There is, of course, no basic touchstone on which to judge the democratic intent of Islamic groups other than to encourage participation and then adopt a policy of 'wait and see'. According to Amatzia Baram:

> since the relations between Islamic and non-Islamic oppositional forces in Iraq thawed in 1990 further cooperation may be expected . . . the longer such cooperation takes place, the more established it becomes and one may expect tolerance to grow. In its turn this may bring about a more democratic outlook.

As Baram rightly states the willingness of Shi'ite fundamentalist movements to form a united front with non-Islamic organizations may suggest 'a step towards a less sectarian, less totalitarian political approach'; but one important factor remains, all these changes are 'still reversible'.[38]

Nevertheless, should a coalition of Islamic and non-Islamic groups decide to act in concert with one another it may be possible for a democratic consociational model of government to develop which could be embraced as both legitimate and representative. G. H. Jansen argues that it is possible to have 'pluralism without democracy'.[39] He is, of course, quite correct; it is also possible to have participation without democracy. But although procedures may not fully correspond with the characteristics of liberal democracy, pluralism and participation are important moves towards a measure of democratization in the Arab world. The next move must surely be in the direction of accountability.

Socio-economic change

As Table 7.2 indicates, Iran, Kuwait, Syria, Jordan and Lebanon made considerable advances in the spheres of educational and health improvements over the past 15–25 years, and their economies have witnessed a shift from the agricultural sector into the service sector. In all countries with the exception of Iran, the breakdown of labour figures for 1985–7 indicate a higher percentage employed within the service sector than in either agricultural or industrial sectors. In Iran the 11 million labour force is more evenly divided between the three sectors. Literacy rates have improved in all countries between 1970 and 1985. According to data from the Iranian Islamic Republic's National Census of Population and Housing, released in 1989, 65 per cent of urban women and 80 per cent of urban men were literate, although rural rates were lower at 60 and 36 per cent for men and women respectively.[40]

The under-five mortality rate dropped significantly across the region between 1960 and 1987. Health and education expenditure did not reach the heights of military expenditure throughout the period but in basic economic trends, the figures suggest a modernizing tendency: a differentiated labour market, invariably reflected in a changing class structure and an increasingly literate population with access to education and healthcare. However, it would be unwise to link democratization too closely with socio-economic determinants. In fact, academics have cautioned that the process of economic modernization may actually produce destabilizing consequences. As Diamond et al. maintain: 'New interests are generated, new consciousness is kindled and new political and organisational capacities are acquired at the individual and group level. Demands multiply both for the right to participate and for tangible and symbolic benefits.' If these are not met, institutions run the risk of breaking down with society lapsing into chaos.[41]

Many analysts have pointed to the rapid and uneven economic development witnessed in the Middle East to be responsible for the societal disorientation and disenchantment which underpinned the rise of and adherence to the ethics and values of Islam.[42] Education has been viewed ambivalently, either feared because it exposes people to alternative ideas or on the grounds that it assists in socializing certain values supportive of the state. Islam has proved a powerful attraction for both the educated and ill-educated although a recent study in Jordan proposes the establishment of a stronger link between democratization and education. The 'Education in the Arab World in the twenty-first century' report looks forward to economic development and political participation taking place, based on the premise that education would become standardized to include the principle freedoms of speech and association.[43] King Hussein of Jordan has announced that courses on democracy will be taught in educational and cultural institutions.

The interesting development occurring recently has been the fact that numerous countries within the region have been discussing economic structures at the same time as political issues. In June 1991 Jordan lifted the ban on political parties and simultaneously emphasized the desire for economic reform and the adoption of policies which would provide: 'an appropriate climate to activate the private sector'. The Amir of Kuwait spoke of the need to 'transfer some activities and services to the private sector' and President Assad commented on Syria operating 'within a framework of economic pluralism' which would secure the 'widest possible participation of citizens in the nation's economic development'. President Hirawi of Lebanon looked forward to an 'economy that encourages private initiative and a free market'.[44]

These statements indicated that economic development would take a more liberalized form. Economic reform, then, would seem to suggest a diminishing role for the state and by implication, the role of the present political leaderships. The corollary of such a move would be some form of political change or readjustment. It is quite possible that the generally acknowledged incompetence and inefficiency of the command economy has been recognized in the Middle East. The 'rentier state' analysis of the 'allocative state' may become inadequate as state structures no longer control a monopoly of economic functions and, therefore, need to accommodate different economic interests. As Rodney Wilson pointed out: 'State owned and run industries were established at huge expense in Syria and Iraq and none of the ventures has achieved commercial viability.'[45]

Democratization in the Third World

The push for democratization, pluralism and multi-partyism in the Third World has recently been viewed as very much linked to the massive shove from the West. The West has set a series of objectives for the developing world, one of which includes encouraging democratization or, the 'concept of good governance'. Governance is an interesting term for it carries the 'unspoken assumption that mere pressure on states to change policies will not work because these states are not able to implement such policies'.[46] Therefore, World Bank initiatives are linked to tutelage in appropriate forms of good government. Tom Young suggests that governance will become increasingly focused on 'freedom, rights and possibly civil society' and points to the example of Mozambique which 'precisely because of its desperate weakness, is being subjected to a degree of remodelling without precedent . . . in which a fundamentally liberal vision is being imposed on a Third World society to which it is almost wholly foreign'.[47] Conversely, an alternative view argues that whilst political democracy might be welcome in southern Africa, the forced multi-party hybrid at the behest of the World Bank's structural adjustment programme is undesirable and will probably work to the advantage of elites' interests thus preventing the 'adoption of policies in the immediate interests of the majority'. The prognosis is not good: 'The only difference will be that whereas in the 1970s and 1980s appeals to economic liberation and socialism provided the smoke-screen behind which the few enriched themselves, in the 1990s the rhetoric will be that of markets, "trickle-down" and multi-party democracy'.[48] In short, then, democratization is either unsuitable and artificial or inequitable and elitist.

Undoubtedly, there exists an international agenda aimed at democratization in Third World states. In 1984 the United States created an agency 'expressly to promote democracy abroad', the National Endowment for Democracy, which is funded through appropriations from the United States Congress. Its main objective is to 'assist democrats, especially in undemocratic countries'.[49] The underlying motivation is 'what is good for democracy is good for America. The more democratic the world becomes, the more likely it is to be both peaceful and friendly to America.'[50] These views may seem fanciful and far removed from previous policy proposals. In the past, the emphasis of the West has been on maintaining order and stability in the Third World rather than encouraging what was seen as disruptive democracy. Yet according to reports in 1990 calls emanated from across the African continent for the institution of multi-party political systems; calls which were endorsed by Western governments, aid donors and lending institutions.[51] The Organization of African Unity proclaimed in 1990 the necessity to 'democratise further our societies and consolidate democratic institutions'. The catalyst for change came from the political changes taking place in Eastern and Central Europe, and in various quarters there was talk of a new climate of opinion developing in a more democratic direction throughout Africa and other Third World countries.

Critics, however, were dubious of the similarities drawn between Eastern Europe and African states, pointing to the fact that multi-party politics had actually been tried and tested in a number of developing states over twenty years' ago and had been found wanting.[52] Multi-party politics had degenerated into tribal politics which then promoted inter-ethnic tension. In short, states in the Third World had a taste of multi-partyism, did not like it and, therefore, it was unlikely to be more palatable now. The prospect of pluralistic, liberal democratic modes of political expression being embraced by or forced upon developing states raised the spectre of past patterns of political experience and the same predictions of doom. In a sense, the arguments returned to those views expressed by early writers disappointed with the post-independent experience of numerous countries. The question posed by Lucien Pye nearly thirty years ago resurfaced: was liberal democracy unsuited for developing nations? The answer was a resounding yes, particularly if it was to be foisted on Third World states through external pressure. There would be a drift to violence and one academic mused: 'There is absolutely no reason why history should not repeat itself . . . multi-partyism by 1995 to be followed by de facto one-party rule by 2000 would seem a good guess.'[53]

Liberal democratic modes of government were still judged to be inappropriate for developing nations. Chazan et al. maintained that by comparison with the political consolidation of Europe, 'The African states have only travelled a short distance toward solving the enormous problems of state and nation-building . . . State capabilities for penetrating society and carrying into effect policies decided at the centre remain weak; government is often characterised by personal rule.'[54]

So, where does the Middle East 'fit' in the picture of Third World democratization? Is the prospect for multi-party pluralism as barren as it is

Table 7.3 Media communications

Iran	Population 53 million; 51% live in urban areas 10 million radios; 2 million TVs. Radio relay systems extends throughout the country
Iraq	Population 17.6 million; 70% live in urban areas 2.2 million radios; 600,000 TVs
Jordan	Population 2.8 million; 66% live in urban areas 1 million radios; 250,000 TVs; 125,000 are colour TVs
Kuwait	Population 2 million; 93% live in urban areas 500,000 radios; 500,000 TVs
Syria	Population 12 million; 49% live in urban areas 2.5 million radios; 600,000 TVs. Fair telecommunications system
Lebanon	Population 3 million; 83% live in urban areas 2 million radios; 800,000 TVs. Tele-Liban is a multi-channel commercial service
Israel	Population 4.4 million; 89% live in urban areas 1.5 million Palestinians. 3 million radios; 1 million TVs

Source: *ITN Fact book* (London, 1990)

perceived to be in other developing nations? Or are there special features peculiar to the region which have somehow retarded democratic progression? Economic factors in the region might appear conducive to some form of democratization, as would the level of communication, although of course there are differences between states (see Table 7.3). Islam is a major factor in balancing any moves towards liberal democracy, but it is a force which is not confined to the region and has penetrated way beyond the boundaries of the Middle Eastern states. Two important issues, however, have contributed to political debility in the region, namely the related areas of population mobility and citizenship. There can be little doubt that these two elements pose a significant threat to national integration and associated political reforms. Yet, in a curious way these issues are not, of themselves, solely features of underdevelopment or, indeed, concerns which are confined to the Third World.

Problems of nationalism, national integration/disintegration, ethnicity, population mobility and citizenship are now, in the post-Cold War international environment, confronting the successor states of the Soviet Union, central and eastern Europe. When countries, developed or non-developed, are exposed to certain conditions, problems of instability and governmental breakdown appear. Whereas in the past the Third World debate informed and instructed us of the differentials between the categories of First, Second and Third Worlds, it may now be time to change our perspective, as issues which wrought the Third World become increasingly prominent elsewhere. We may within the next decade speak of the Islamic world which will demand a wider, multi-regional approach.

Is democratization, or talk of democratization, a sham in the Middle East? It is obviously too premature to judge. Diamond et al. found in their comparative study of democracy in developing nations that the one common thread which consistently reappeared was 'the crucial importance of effective and democratically committed leadership'.[55] Although any emphasis on the role of leadership tends to stress the importance of elite groups, they argue, that corrupt, opportunistic and undemocratic practice of leaders can seep down the hierarchical structure and inflict damage: 'When a prolonged period of undemocratic or inept leadership is experienced, the system itself may begin to decay.'[56] Certainly, the role of the leadership is important in the Middle Eastern states simply on the grounds of their political structures and their general authoritarian frameworks. In the traditional monarchies/dynasties 'the powers of rule-making, rule application and even central adjudication are merged in the head of the state'.[57] Even the Ba'ath Party had 'radically changed its nature' over the past 20 to 30 years of power in Iraq and Syria. From a party with an overt military presence in the early years of rule it has become a party very much linked to a 'cult of personality'.[58] This tendency has led to higher political profiles for the leadership, Saddam Hussein and President Assad. In the case of Iraq, it was widely acknowledged during the 1991 Gulf War that despite Saddam Hussein's attraction to wearing uniforms he, in fact, had no military background and used the Iraqi military to serve his own interests. In the case of Syria, Assad has played down the role of the military by gradually enhancing his personal role in the political affairs of the country.

It is apparent that the leadership in the Middle East has raised the question of democracy. When President Assad stated: 'The democratic form is not a commodity that is imported from this or that country but it is the framework through which the citizens practise their rights and duties', he is quite correct, but unless the dominant role of the Ba'ath Party is minimized through constitutional amendment, his words appear vacuous.[59] There are few ways of assessing the public sentiment of countries within the region except through the conduit of demonstrations and riots. Although, one could interpret the discernible shift away from the Ba'ath Party in favour of the Independents at recent elections in Syria to suggest a strong disenchantment with the party and, indeed, the leadership. However, these moves will find little potency unless the disparities between the parties competing in elections is changed. If King Hussein's dictum that 'one-party rule, political armies, dictatorships and autocracies are all things of the past', is to have any real meaning, words will have to be turned into action.[60]

The leadership in the Middle East may, of course, feel obliged to make democratic statements because of international pressure and this may have resulted in King Hussein's decision to reintroduce elections; a move directed by the structural adjustment programmes of the World Bank. In this sense, certain states in the region share external pressures with many African states, but there had been demonstrations and demands for the establishment of democratic government in Jordan for some considerable time. In other words, there may be external pressure to democratize, but correspondingly there may be internal pressures too; the two elements are not mutually exclusive.

The most difficult question, as yet unanswered definitively, is whether liberal democracy is desired in the Middle East. According to one analyst, the Arab states reject the democratic option 'because of where it comes from rather than what it contains'.[61] It may not be surprising and perhaps inevitable, that the Arab states should resent the West and not wish to emulate liberal democratic political structures. But it must be remembered that unlike their Third World counterparts who have become increasingly indebted to the West, the Middle Eastern countries have had the power through massive oil wealth to create a new economic order. When the Arab Gulf states are congratulated for successfully managing their funds it is precisely because they have recycled their petro-dollars into investments in international financial markets and real estate in the West. It might seem contradictory to fully participate in the capitalist economies of the West, whilst continuing to reject their underlying political systems.

Other academics maintain that 'democracy, liberty and political parties do not carry the same connotations in the Arab world as they do in the West'. The Arab states find themselves at a crossroads, Janus-faced, looking towards modernity and tradition.[62] In this sense, the Middle East's alleged ambivalence to liberal democracy and the sensitivity to the fact that it is a Western concept may reflect fears which are being expressed about the suitability of liberal democracy in the wider Third World. However, one fundamental and encouraging sign is the fact that a debate about democratization has begun and this is exceptionally important in a region where, in the past, governmental change if it took place at all was largely a familial affair or wrought with violence and repression. As Esposito and Piscatori point out, modes of political expression are not static:

> It is difficult to ascertain or to predict whether the evolution of Muslim thinking about democracy will lead them to convert their views into action and what particular form democratisation might take in diverse Muslim cultures. It is clear, however, that in the new Muslim world order, Muslim political traditions and institutions are evolving, just as social conditions and class structures are changing. Both are important for the future of democracy in the Middle East.[63]

One aspect is quite clear, the ending of the Cold War has created a new environment in which states in the Middle East may enjoy, not only, new possibilities of political autonomy, but also, and perhaps more significantly, greater demands for responsibility and accountability. In a sense, the onus is now on the states of the region to define and determine their political progress in a democratic direction. Through discussion, the re-introduction of elections and greater political participation the first tentative steps have been taken on the road to a fuller and more expressive form of democracy. As history reminds us, those first moves towards democratization are often the hardest.

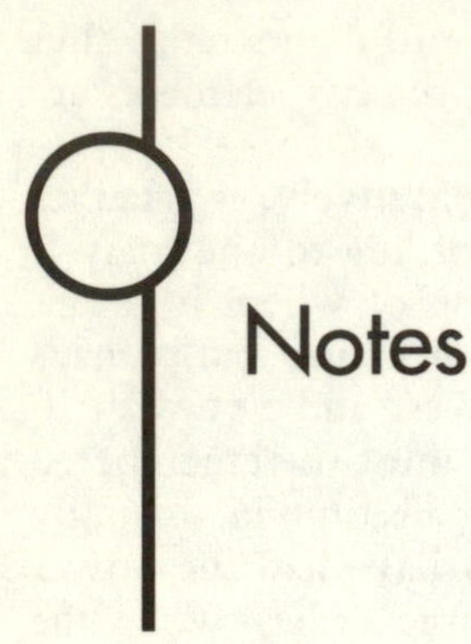

Notes

1 Democracy and democratization

1 J. S. Mill, *Considerations of Representative Government* (London, n.d.) p. 126.
2 J. Schumpeter, *Capitalism, Socialism and Democracy* (London, 1957) p. 285.
3 R. Dahl, *A Preface to Democratic Theory* (Chicago, 1956) p. 86.
4 J. S. Mill, op. cit. p. 68.
5 Ibid., p. 44.
6 Ibid., p. 300.
7 Ibid., p. 217.
8 Ibid., p. 168.
9 R. Berelson, 'Survival through apathy', in *Frontiers of Democratic Theory*, Henry Kariel (ed.) (New York, 1970) p. 69.
10 Cf. G. Duncan and S. Lukes, 'Democracy restated', in Kariel (ed.), op. cit., pp. 189–91; B. Berelson, P. Lazarfeld and W. McPhee, *Voting* (Chicago, 1954); Dahl, op. cit.; Schumpeter, op. cit.
11 J. Schumpeter, 'Democracy as elite competition', in Kariel (ed.), op. cit., p. 40.
12 Ibid.
13 S. M. Lipset, *Political Man* (London, 1966) p. 71.
14 G. A. Almond and James S. Coleman (eds), *The Politics of the Developing Areas* (Princeton, 1960).
15 R. Ward and D. Rustow (eds), *Political Modernisation in Japan and Turkey* (Princeton, 1964) p. 7; Karl Deutsch, 'Social mobilisation and political development', in C. Welch (ed.) *Political Modernisation* (Belmont, 1967) p. 153.
16 Daniel Lerner, *The Passing of Traditional Society* (Glencoe, 1958) pp. 48–50.
17 G. Almond and S. Verba, *The Civic Culture* (Princeton, 1963) p. 4; Frederick W. Frey, 'Political development, power and communications in Turkey', in L. Pye (ed.), *Communications and Political Development* (Princeton, 1963) p. 301.
18 Lucien Pye, 'Democracy, modernisation and nation building', in J. R. Pennock (ed.), *Self Government in Modernising Nations* (New Jersey, 1964) p. 7.
19 Ibid., p. 10.
20 S. Huntington, 'Political development and political decay', in Welch (ed.), op. cit., p. 241.

21 Ibid., p. 245.
22 Ibid.; Myron Weiner, 'Political integration and political development', in C. Welch (ed.), op. cit., p. 188.
23 W. Kornhauser, *The Politics of Mass Society* (New York, 1957) p. 125.
24 V. Randall and R. Theobalds, *Political Change and Underdevelopment: A Critical Introduction to Third World Politics* (London, 1985) p. 69.
25 S. Huntington, 'Political development and political decay', in Welch (ed.), op. cit. pp. 276–77.
26 Ibid., p. 251.
27 C. B. Macpherson, *Democratic Theory – Essays in Retrieval* (Oxford, 1973) p. 190.
28 Ibid., p. 191.
29 Ibid., pp. 162–5.
30 Ibid., p. 158.
31 Richard Joseph, *Democracy and Prebendal Politics in Nigeria. The Rise and Fall of the Second Republic* (Cambridge, 1987) p. 20.
32 S. M. Lipset, op. cit., p. 71.
33 *Financial Times*, 13 August 1990; BBC Summary of World Broadcasts; (issued by BBC Monitoring) Middle East (SWB ME)/1174 A/5, 11 September 1991.
34 L. Diamond, J. Linz and S. M. Lipset, *Democracy in Developing Countries*, Vol. 3 (London, 1989); N. Chazan, R. Mortimer, J. Ravenhill, and D. Rothchild, *Politics and Society in Contemporary Africa* (Boulder, 1988); Colin Stoneman, *Political Democracy: Necessary but not Sufficient for Development in South Africa*, New England College, May 1992.
35 Diamond et al., Ibid.
36 G. Luciani, *The Arab State* (London, 1990) p. xxiv.
37 *Middle East International*, 13 September 1991.
38 SWB ME/1329 A/4, 14 March 1992.
39 SWB ME/1213 A/6, 26 October 1991.
40 SWB ME/1334 A.12, 20 March 1992; SWB ME/1323 A/9, 7 March 1992.
41 J. Espositio and J. Piscatori, 'Democratisation and Islam', *Middle East Journal*, Vol. 45, No. 3, 1991; M. Hudson, 'After the Gulf War: prospects for democratisation in the Arab World', *Middle East Journal*, Vol. 45, No. 3, 1991.
42 Herman van Gunsteren, 'Notes on a theory of citizenship', in P. Birnbaum, J. Lively and G. Parry (eds) *Democracy, Consensus and Social Contract* (London, 1978) p. 9.
43 Sharon Stanton Russell, 'Migration and political integration in the Arab world', in G. Luciani, op. cit., p. 377.
44 van Gunsteren, op. cit., p. 10.
45 Parry, 'Citizenship and Knowledge', Ibid. p. 40.
46 Kornhauser, op. cit., p. 45.
47 Ibid., p. 55.
48 Russell, op. cit., p. 378.
49 M. Al-Rumiaihi, Royal Institute for International Affairs, Chatham House, London, May 1991. (See Chapter 2 for details of Kuwait's political structure.)
50 Russell, op. cit., p. 381.
51 Ibid., p. 380.
52 Ibid.
53 SWB ME/1213 A/7, 26 October 1991.
54 See Chapter 2 for details of Jordan's political structure.
55 Mill, op. cit., p. 69.
56 Arend Lijphart, *Democracy in Plural Societies – A Comparative Exploration* (New Haven, 1977) p. 1.

57 Ibid., p. 145.
58 David Poole, 'Democratisation and its limits in the Middle East', *Political Studies Association*, April 1991, pp. 7–8.
59 Peter Bachrach and Morton S. Baratz, in Kariel (ed.) op. cit., p. 269, cf. Lijphart, op. cit., p. 50.
60 Lijphart, ibid., p. 50.
61 Ibid. p. 52.
62 Lipset, op. cit., pp. 46–7.
63 J. Piscatori, *Islam in a World of Nation States* (Cambridge, 1986); G. W. Choudhury *Islam and the Contemporary World* (London, 1990); Leonard Binder, *Islamic Liberalism* (Chicago, 1988); Akbar S. Ahmed, *Postmodernism and Islam: Predicament and Promise* (London, 1992).
64 Piscatori, ibid. p. 24.
65 Choudhury, op. cit., p. iii.
66 Ibid.
67 Ibid., p. 45.
68 Ibid., p. ii.
69 Ami Ayalon, *Language and Change in the Arab Middle East* (Oxford, 1987) p. 121.
70 Ahmed, op. cit., p. 264.

2 The monarchical/dynastic state – Jordan and Kuwait

1 SWB ME/1213 A/6, 26 October 1991.
2 SWB ME/1104 A/5, 21 June 1991.
3 M. Hudson, *Arab Politics* (New Haven, 1977) p. 212.
4 Major John Bagot Glubb became Arab Legion commander on the eve of the Second World War. He was ordered to leave the country on 1 March 1956.
5 Aims of Palestine Mandate:

   1 The incorporation of the whole of the Balfour Declaration.
   2 The recognition of the 'historical connection of the Jewish people with Palestine'.
   3 The facilitation of Jewish immigration and the 'close settlement by Jews on the land', provided that the 'Mandatory ensures the rights and position of other sections of the population are not prejudiced'. F. J. Khouri, *The Arab Israeli Dilemma* (New York, 1977) p. 16.

6 M. Wilson, *King Abdullah, Britain and the Making of Jordan* (London, 1987); Avi Schlaim *The Politics of Partition* (London, 1990); B. Morris, *The Birth of the Palestinian Refugee Problem, 1947–9* (Cambridge, 1987).
7 United Nations Report on Palestine 1990, United Nations Information Centre (London, 1991).
8 S. S. Russell, 'Migration and political integration in the Arab world', in G. Luciani, *The Arab State* (London, 1990) p. 375.
9 United Nations Report, op. cit.
10 World Zionist Organization, *Kivunim*, February 1982.
11 *Jerusalem Post*, 27 June 1982.
12 *Middle East International*, 8 August 1986.
13 *Middle East and North Africa* (London, 1990) p. 540.
14 Resolution of Conference of Arab Heads of State, Rabat, 28 October 1974, in ibid. p. 77.
15 Philip Robins, *Middle East International,* 22 February 1985.
16 Peter Gubser, *Politics and Change in Al-Karak*, Jordan (London, 1973) p. 177.

17 Ibid., pp. 167–72.
18 *Middle East International,* 28 April 1989.
19 'Reagan Plan', in *Middle East and North Africa* (London, 1990) pp. 83–4.
20 *Middle East International*, 7 March 1986.
21 *Middle East and North Africa*, op cit., p. 546.
22 *Middle East Economic Digest,* 5 August 1988.
23 *Middle East International,* 26 August 1988.
24 *ITN Factbook* (London, 1990).
25 Akbar S. Ahmed, *Postmodernism and Islam: Predicament and Promise* (London, 1992) p. 223.
26 *Keesings Record of World Events*, Vol. 35, November 1989, p. 37502.
27 *Middle East International*, 6 December 1985.
28 SWB ME/1213 A/7, 26 October 1991.
29 *Keesings Record of World Events*, Vol. 37, February 1991, p. 38024.
30 SWB ME/1104 A/5, 21 June 1991.
31 SWB ME/1272 A/11, 8 January 1992.
32 SWB ME/1237 A/7, 23 November 1991.
33 Ibrahim Bakr, 'The Palestinian Writer', in *The Guardian*, 20 August 1990.
34 M. Hudson, op. cit., p. 185.
35 Ahmed Al-Khatib, 'Prospects for Political Change in Kuwait', Royal Institute of International Affairs, Chatham House, London, May 1991.
36 M. Al-Rumaihi, Rebuilding Kuwait and Socio-Economic Change After the Occupation, Royal Institute of International Affairs, Chatham House, London, May 1991.
37 *Middle East and North Africa*, op. cit., p. 587.
38 Luciani, op. cit., pp. 75–6.
39 Ahmed Al-Khatib, op. cit.
40 *Middle East International*, 8 August 1986.
41 Ibid., 11 July 1986.
42 *Keesings Record of World Events*, Vol. 35, September 1989, No. 9, p. 36652.
43 *Keesings Record of World Events*, Vol. 36, June 1990, p. 37549.
44 Ibid.
45 Al-Khatib, op. cit.
46 Al-Rumaihi, op. cit.
47 SWB ME/1001, 3 June 1991; *Keesings Record of World Events*, Vol. 37, June 1991, p. 38309.
48 Hudson, op. cit., p. 185.
49 *The Guardian,* 31 July 1992.

3 The theocratic state – Iran

1 T. Mostyn, *Iran, Iraq and the Arabian Peninsular 1945–1990* (London, 1991).
2 *Middle East and North Africa* (Europa, 1990) p. 421.
3 C. D. Carr, 'The US-Iranian relationship, 1948–1978: a study in reverse influence', in Hossein Amirsadeghi, *The Security of the Persian Gulf* (London, 1981) p. 60.
4 Ibid.
5 M. Reza Ghods, *Iran in the 20th Century* (London, 1990) p. 192; S. Huntington, '*Political Development and Political* Decay', in C. Welch (ed.) *Political Modernisation* (Belmont, 1967).
6 Carr, op. cit., p. 67.
7 Mostyn, op. cit., p. 75.

8 Reza Ghods, op. cit., p. 191.
9 Mostyn, op. cit., p. 130.
10 Bager Moin, *Khomeini* (London, 1989).
11 Mostyn, op. cit., p. 83.
12 Reza Ghods, op. cit., p. 195.
13 Ibid., p. 208.
14 Martin Wright (ed.), *Iran, The Khomeini Revolution* (London, 1989) p. 19.
15 Ibid.
16 Cited in D. Peretz, *The Middle East Today* (New York, 1983) p. 512.
17 Reza Ghods, op. cit.
18 D. Rustow, 'The politics of the Near East', in G. Almond and J. Coleman (eds), *The Politics of the Developing Areas* (Princeton, 1960) p. 425.
19 Martin Wright, op. cit., p. 924.
20 Ibid.
21 A. Al-Azmah, 'Prospects for Democracy in the Arab World', St Hugh's College, Oxford, 15 June 1991.
22 John Voll, 'Islamic fundamentalism' in H. Maull and O. Pick (ed.) *The Gulf War* (London, 1989) p. 34; Akbar S. Ahmed, 'Into the 1990s: An Islamic Perspective', RIIA, Chatham House, 10 May 1991; A. Ahmed, *Postmodernism and Islam* (London, 1992).
23 *Keesings Record of World Events*, December 1990, Vol. 35, No. 12, p. 37929.
24 *Middle East International,* 6 January 1989.
25 Cited in D. Peretz, op. cit., p. 512.
26 *Middle East International,* 6 December 1985.
27 *Keesings Record of World Events*, April 1990, Vol. 36, No. 4, p. 37422.
28 *ITN Factbook* (London, 1990).
29 Alan Taylor, *Middle East International,* 6 December 1985.
30 *Keesings Record of World Events*, July 1989, Vol. 35, No. 7, p. 36833.
31 SWB ME/1255 A/5, 14 December 1991.
32 L. Diamond, J. Linz and S. M. Lipset (eds), *Democracy in Developing Countries, Vol. 3.* (London, 1989) p. 8.
33 Shahram Chubin, 'Iran and the War', in Maull and Pick, op. cit., p. 7.
34 SWB ME/1093 A/8, 8 June 1991.
35 SWB ME/1155 A/4, 20 August 1991.
36 Ibid.
37 Kamal Kharrazi, 'Perspectives on the Future of the Region', RIIA, Chatham House, 10 May 1991.
38 *Middle East International,* 31 March 1989.
39 SWB ME/1199 A/4, 10 October 1991.
40 Choudhury, *Islam and the Contemporary World* (London, 1990) p. 115.
41 Ibid.
42 Leonard Binder, *Islamic Liberalism* (Chicago, 1988) p. 357.
43 Ibid.
44 Arnold Toynbee, *The World and the West* (London, 1953) p. 15.

4 The dominant party state – Syria and Iraq

1 S. Huntington, 'Political development and political decay' in C. Welch (ed.), *Political Modernisation* (Belmont, 1967) p. 272.
2 Translation of Official Ba'ath Party document: 'Analysis of Sectarianism, Regionalism and Tribalism', April 1966, in N. Van Dam, *The Struggle for Power in Syria* (London, 1979) p. 104.

3 Ibid., p. 109.
4 Fuad Khuri, 'Social Conditions and Democracy', St Hugh's College, Oxford. 15 June 1991; D. Rustow, 'Politics of the Near East', in J. Coleman and G. Almond (eds), *The Politics of the Developing Areas* (Princeton, 1960) p. 413.
5 *Middle East and North Africa* (London, 1990) p. 792.
6 Ibid.
7 SWB M/E 1213 A/5. Iraqi News Agency, 23 April 1989.
8 *Keesings Record of World Events*, September 1990, Vol. 36, No. 9, p. 37753.
9 M. Ma'oz and A. Yaniv, *Syria Under Assad* (London, 1986) p. 33.
10 Michael C. Hudson, *Arab Politics* (New Haven, 1977) p. 64.
11 Ibid., p. 63.
12 Van Dam, op. cit., p. 102.
13 Ibid.
14 Speech by President Assad, 18 August 1977, in Ma'oz and Yaniv, op. cit., p. 93.
15 *Middle East International*, 25 January 1985.
16 *Middle East International*, 4 May 1984.
17 *Keesings Record of World Events*, September 1990, Vol. 36, No. 9, p. 37753.
18 See Chapter 6 for details.
19 SWB ME/1075 A/16, 18 May 1991.
20 SWB ME/1233 A/12, 19 November 1991.
21 *Middle East International*, 11 October 1991.
22 Hudson, op. cit., p. 265.
23 M. Farouk and P. Sluglett, 'The Iraqi Ba'ath Party', in Vicky Randall (ed.) *Political Parties in the Third World* (London, 1988) p. 73.
24 A. Darwish and G. Alexander, *Unholy Babylon* (London, 1991) p. 211.
25 M. Farouk Sluglett and P. Sluglett 'Labour and national liberation. The trade union movement in Iraq 1920–1958', *Arab Studies Quarterly*, Vol. 5, No. 2, 1981, p. 145.
26 M. Farouk and P. Sluglett, *Iraq since 1958* (London, 1990) p. 93.
27 Cited in *Committee Against Repression and for Democratic Rights in Iraq. Saddam's Iraq* (CAPDR) (London, 1991) p. 211.
28 Darwish and Alexander, op. cit., p. 25; Ibid., p. 32.
29 The 1968 Revolution in Iraq. Political Report of the 8th Congress of the Arab Ba'ath Socialist Party in Iraq, January 1974 (London, 1979) p. 30.
30 Cited in CAPDR, op. cit., p. 31; Hanna Batatu, *The Old Social Classes and the Revolutionary Movements in Iraq* (Princeton, 1978) p. 47.
31 Jean Leca 'Social structure and political stability', in G. Luciani, *The Arab State* (London, 1990) p. 171.
32 M. and P. Sluglett (1990), op. cit., p. 93.
33 The 1968 Revolution in Iraq. Political Report of 8th Congress of the Arab Ba'ath Socialist Party in Iraq, op. cit., p. 11.
34 CAPDR, op. cit., p. 41.
35 The 1968 Revolution in Iraq. Political Report of 8th Congress of the Arab Ba'ath Socialist Party in Iraq, op. cit., p. 11.
36 M. and P. Sluglett (1990), op. cit., p. 117.
37 CAPDR, op. cit., p. 151.
38 Ibid., p. 152.
39 *Middle East and North Africa*, op. cit., p. 486.
40 CAPDR, op. cit., p. 153.
41 M. and P. Sluglett (1990), op. cit., p. 152.
42 CAPDR, op. cit., p. 154.
43 Majid Khadduri, *Socialist Iraq* (Washington, DC, 1978) p. 88.
44 *Middle East and North Africa*, op. cit., p. 482.

45 M. and P. Sluglett (1990), op. cit., p. 186.
46 Daniel Pipes 'A border adrift: origins of the conflict', in S. Tahir-Kheli and S. Ayubi (eds), *Iran/Iraq War: New Weapons Old Conflicts* (New York, 1983) p. 5.
47 *Keesings Contemporary Archives*, 7 November, 1980, p. 30562.
48 CAPDR, op. cit., pp. 172–3.
49 Tareq Y. Ismael, 'Ideology in recent Iraqi foreign policy', in Tahir-Kheli and S. Ayubi (eds), op. cit.; Charles Tripp, BRISMES Meeting, School of Oriental and African Studies, University of London, 10 July 1991.
50 Interview between Saddam Hussein and Fuad Matar, in F. Matar, *Saddam Hussein, The Man, the Cause and the Future* (London, 1981) p. 278.
51 CAPDR, op. cit., p. 166.
52 *Middle East International*, 22 March 1985.
53 M. and P. Sluglett (1990) op. cit.; Fred Halliday, 'Aftermath of the Gulf War', London School of Economics Meeting, June 1991.
54 Patrick Seale, *The Observer*, 2 May 1982.
55 Tim Niblock, 'Prospects for Stability in Iraq', Royal Institute of International Affairs, Chatham House Meeting, London, 10 May 1991.
56 M. and P. Sluglett (1990) p. 241.
57 F. Matar, op. cit., p. 281.
58 *Middle East International*, 22 March 1985.
59 *Keesings Record of World Events*, March 1989, Vol. 35, No. 3, p. 36567.
60 *Keesings Record of World Events*, April 1989, Vol. 35, No. 4, p. 36601.
61 *Middle East International*, 14 April 1989.
62 *Keesings Record of World Events*, April 1989, op. cit.
63 SWB ME/1100 A/3, 17 June 1991.
64 Cf. SWB ME/1195, 15 October 1991; ME/1256, 16 December 1991; ME/1222, 6 November 1991; ME/1225, 9 November 1991.
65 SWB ME/1275 A/6, 11 January 1992.
66 SWB ME/1201 A/12, 12 October 1991.
67 SWB ME/1062 A/2, 2 May 1991.
68 *The Guardian*, 18 July 1991.
69 SWB ME. 1117(i), 6 July 1991.
70 M. al Hashemi Hamdi, *al'Alam Magazine*, 10 July 1991; Tareq Y. Ismael, op. cit.
71 Niblock, op. cit.
72 *Middle East International*, 31 May 1991.
73 *The Guardian*, 18 July 1991.

5 The multi-party state – Israel

1 Jehuda Reinharz, 'The transition from Yishuv to state: social and ideological changes', in L. Silberstein (ed.), *New Perspectives on Israeli History* (New York, 1991) pp. 29–30.
2 *ITN Factbook* (London, 1990) p. 267.
3 Reinharz, op. cit., p. 34.
4 D. Rustow, 'Politics of the Near East', in G. Almond and J. Coleman (eds) *The Politics of the Developing Areas* (Princeton, 1960) p. 385.
5 British/Israel Public Affairs Committee (BIPAC).
6 Ibid.
7 Ghada Kharmi, 'After the Gulf War', Meeting 26 June 1991, London School of Economics.
8 Y. Liebowitz, *Middle East International*, 13 June 1986.

9 SWB ME/1198 A/5, 9 October 1991.
10 David Capitanchick, 'After the Gulf War,' Meeting 26 June 1991, London School of Economics.
11 For precise details of the electoral system see W. Frankel, *Israel Observed* (London, 1980) pp. 19–30.
12 J. Bara, 'Alignment and de-alignment; aspects of electoral politics in Israel in 1980s and 1990s', *Political Studies Association*, April 1991.
13 Ibid. p. 19.
14 Haim Baram, *Middle East International*, 3 May 1985.
15 Massada was the scene of a massacre of Jewish people in the first millennium.
16 Ilan Baruch, Political Counsellor, Israeli Embassy, 'After the Gulf War', Meeting 26 June 1991, London School of Economics.
17 *Jerusalem Post*, 24 March 1990.
18 A. Arien, 'The Israeli electorate, 1977', in A. Arien (ed.) *The Elections in Israel, 1977* (Jerusalem, 1980) p. 271.
19 Israel Shahak, *Middle East International*, 15 June 1984.
20 Ibid.
21 D. Capitanchik, in J. Bara, op. cit., p. 11; Benny Morris, *The Birth of the Palestinian Refugee Problem 1947–1949* (Cambridge, 1987).
22 *Middle East International*, 29 April 1983.
23 SWB ME/1198 A/5, 9 October 1991.
24 J. Bara, op. cit., p. 12.
25 *Jerusalem Post*, 25 November 1990.
26 Israkit, British/Israel Public Affairs Committee, F.14a.
27 *Keesings Records of World Events*, Vol. 36, No. 1, January 1990, p. 37199.
28 *The Guardian*, 2 August 1991.
29 Abraham Ashkenasi, 'Opinion Trends Among Jerusalem Palestinians', *Policy Studies Paper 36*. Leonard Davis Institute, Hebrew University, Jerusalem. *Middle East International*, 26 August 1988.
30 *Keesings Records of World Events*, Vol. 37, No. 2, February 1991, p. 38024.
31 Interview. Jerusalem, 24 November 1990.
32 *The Independent*, 15 November 1991.
33 SWB ME/1214 (i), 28 October 1991; SWB ME/1242 A/2, 29 November 1991; SWB ME/1289 A/1, 28 January 1992.
34 *Middle East International*, 6 March 1992; *Jerusalem Post*, 22 March 1991.
35 *Middle East International*, 6 March 1992.
36 SWB ME/1319 A/15, 3 March 1992.
37 Ibid.

6 The confessional state – the Lebanon

1 S. Huntington, 'Political development and political decay', in C. Welch (ed.), *Political Modernisation* (Belmont, 1967).
2 T. Y. Ismael, *Governments and Politics of the Contemporary Middle East* (Ontario, 1970) p. 234.
3 David Gilmour, *Lebanon. The Fractured Country* (London 1983) p. x.
4 Ismael, op. cit., p. 236.
5 B. M. Borthwick, *Comparative Politics of the Middle East* (New Jersey, 1980) p. 130.
6 Ibid. p. 131; Gilmour, op. cit.; J. Bulloch, *Death of a Country* (London, 1977) p. 9.
7 Fuad Khuri, 'Social Conditions and Democracy', St Hugh's, Oxford, June 1991.

8 Ibid.
9 Weiner, 'Political integration and political development', in Welch (ed.), op. cit., p. 181.
10 Gilmour, op. cit., p. 34.
11 Ibid. p. 35.
12 Ismael, op. cit., p. 237.
13 Borthwick, op. cit., p. 142.
14 Gilmour, op. cit., p. 39.
15 M. Hudson, 'The electoral process and political development in Lebanon', *Middle East Journal*, Vol. 20, No. 2, 1966; Ismael, op. cit.
16 Weiner, op. cit., p. 181.
17 Bulloch, op. cit., p. 1.
18 Robert Fisk, *Pity the Nation* (Oxford, 1990) p. 77.
19 *Middle East International*, 22 March 1985.
20 *Middle East International*, 10 February 1984.
21 *Al-Qabas* (*Kuwaiti Daily*), 13 February 1984.
22 *Middle East International*, 27 July 1984.
23 *Middle East International*, 1 June 1984.
24 *Al-Hawadith*, Editorial, 6 September 1987.
25 *Middle East and North Africa*, (London, 1990) p. 606.
26 As-Safir, 27 September 1988.
27 *ITN Factbook* (London, 1990).
28 SWB ME/1076 A/12, 20 May 1991.
29 SWB ME/1076 A/12, 20 May 1991.
30 SWB ME/1080 A/5, 24 May 1991.
31 Major General Antoine Lahad, Commander of South Lebanon, SWB ME/1082 A/12, 27 May 1991.
32 SWB ME/1082 A/13, 27 May 1991.
33 *The Economist*, 28 September 1991.
34 SWB ME/1080 A/5, 24 May 1991.
35 *The Guardian*, 25 August 1992.

7 Prospects for democracy

1 V. Randall and R. Theobalds, *Political Change and Underdevelopment: A Critical Introduction to Third World Politics* (London, 1985); C. Clapham, *Third World Politics* (London, 1985); P. Cammack, D. Poole and W. Tordoff, *Third World Politics* (London, 1988); N. Chazan, R. Mortimer, J. Ravenhill and D. Rothchild, *Politics and Society in Contemporary Africa* (Colorado, 1988); L. Diamond, J. Linz and S. M. Lipset, *Democracy in Developing Countries*, Vol. 3 (London, 1989).
2 Cammack, et al., op. cit., p. 3.
3 Ibid.
4 Clapham, op. cit., p. 5.
5 Cammack et al., op. cit., p. 4.
6 Ergun Ozbudin, 'Turkey: crises, interruptions and re-equilibrations', in Diamond et al., op. cit., p. 190.
7 D. McDowall, *Middle East International*, 15 May 1992.
8 Cammack et al., op. cit., p. 34.
9 E. Lauterpacht, C. B. Greenwood, Marc Weller and Daniel Bethlehem (eds) The Kuwait Crisis; Basic Documents. Cambridge International Documents Series, Vol. 1 (Cambridge, 1991) p. 74.

10 C. Gertz, 'The integrative revolution: primordial sentiments and civic politics in the new states', in C. Welch, (ed.), *Political Modernisation* (Belmont, 1987) p. 201.
11 J. Muravchik, *Exporting Democracy* (Washington, DC, 1991) p. 119.
12 Ibid.
13 D. Rustow, 'Politics of the Near East', in G. A. Almond and James S. Coleman (eds), *The Politics of the Developing Areas* (Princeton, 1960).
14 United Nations Relief and Works Agency figures for 1991, cited in SWB ME/1213 A/6, 26 October 1991.
15 See Chapter 5.
16 SWB ME/1343 A/1, 31 March 1992.
17 Cf. M. Weiner, 'Political integration and political development', in Welch, op. cit., p. 181; Karl W. Deutsch, *Nationalism and Social Communication* (New York, 1953).
18 Gertz, op. cit., p. 198.
19 Zehra F. Arat, *Democracy and Human Rights in Developing Countries* (Colorado, 1991) p. 129.
20 S. Huntington, 'Political development and political decay', in C. Welch (ed.), *Political Modernisation* (Belmont, 1967) p. 250.
21 Ibid. p. 251.
22 Y. Choueiri, St Hugh's, Oxford, June 1991.
23 Y. Choueiri, *Islamic Fundamentalism* (London, 1990).
24 A. Al-Azmah, 'Islam and Democracy', St Hugh's, Oxford, June 1991.
25 *Middle East International*, 29 May l992.
26 Ibid.; J. L. Espositio and J. Piscatori, 'Democratisation and Islam', *Middle East Journal* Vol. 45, No. 3, 1991.
27 *Middle East International*, 29 May 1992.
28 SWB ME/1353 (i), 11 April 1992.
29 Choueiri, op. cit., p. 160.
30 Al-Azmah, op. cit.
31 Daniel Brumberg, 'Islamic fundamentalism, democracy and the Gulf crisis', in J. Piscatori (ed.), *Islamic Fundamentalism and the Gulf Crisis* (Chicago, 1991) p. 206.
32 Choueiri, op. cit., p. 160.
33 SWB ME/1274 A/6, 10 January 1992.
34 J. Schumpeter in H. Kariel, op cit., p. 40.
35 SWB ME/1314 A/11, 26 February 1992.
36 SWB ME/1314 A/10, 26 February 1992; Amatzia Baram, 'From radicalism to radical pragmatism: the Shi'ite fundamentalist opposition movements of Iraq', in J. Piscatori (ed.), *Islamic Fundamentalism and the Gulf Crisis* (Chicago, 1991) p. 48.
37 Baram op. cit., p. 43.
38 Ibid. pp. 48–9.
39 *Middle East International*, 29 May 1992.
40 V. Moghadam, 'Women, work and ideology in the Islamic Republic', *International Journal of Middle East Studies*, Vol. 20, 1988.
41 Diamond et al., op cit., p. 34.
42 Cf. Fred Halliday and Hamza Alavi (eds), *State and Ideology in the Middle East and Pakistan* (London, 1988) pp. 39–41; Alexander Cudsi and Ali H. Dessouki, *Islam and Power* (London, 1981) p. 193.
43 Georges Zouain UNESCO, 'Education and Democracy', St Hugh's, Oxford.
44 SWB ME/1343 A/1, 31 March 1992; SWB ME/1104 A/3, 21 June 1991; SWB ME/1233 A/12, 19 November 1991; SWB ME/1341 A/6, 28 March 1992.
45 Rodney Wilson, 'Prospects for Economic Revival in the Middle East after the Gulf War', New England College, May 1992.

46 Tom Young, 'Forcing Men to Be Free? Making Sense of the West's Agenda in the Third World: The Case of Mozambique', New England College, May 1992.
47 Ibid.
48 Colin Stoneman, 'Political Democracy: Necessary But Not Sufficient for Development in Southern Africa', New England College, May 1992.
49 Muravchik, op. cit., p. 204.
50 Ibid. p. 222.
51 *Financial Times*, 13 August 1990.
52 S. Decalo, 'Beyond autocracy and state-managerialism in Africa: prospects for the future', in *African Governance in the 1990s: Objectives, Resources and Constraints* (Working Papers for the Inaugural Seminar of the Governance in Africa Program, The Carter Center of Emory University, Atlanta, Georgia, 23–25 March 1990), pp. 191–9.
53 Jeff Haynes, 'The search for democracy in Sub-Sahara Africa', *Political Studies Association*, 1991.
54 Chazan et al., op. cit., p. 141.
55 Diamond et al., op. cit., p. 49.
56 Ibid.
57 Rustow op. cit., p. 447.
58 M. Farouk-Sluglett and P. Sluglett 'The Iraqi Ba'ath Party', in V. Randall (ed.), *Political Parties in the Third World* (London, 1988) p. 72.
59 SWB ME/1329 A/3, 14 March 1992.
60 SWB ME/1314 A/11, 26 February 1992.
61 George Joffe, 'Democracy in the Maghreb', New England College, May 1992.
62 Abd Al-Aziz Duri, 'Historical perspectives', St Hugh's, Oxford, op. cit.
63 Espositio and Piscatori, op. cit., p. 440.

References

Akbar, S. (1992) *Ahmed Postmodernism and Islam: Predicament and Promise*, London, Routledge.

Almond, G. A. and Coleman, J. S. (eds) (1960) *The Politics of the Developing Areas*, Princeton, NJ, Princeton University Press.

Almond, G. A. and Verba, S. (1963) *The Civic Culture*, Princeton, NJ, Princeton University Press.

Amirsadeghi, H. (1981) *The Security of the Persian Gulf*, London, Croom Helm.

Arat, Z. F. (1991) *Democracy and Human Rights in Developing Countries*, Boulder, CO, Lynne Rienner.

Arien, A. (ed.) (1980) *The Elections in Israel 1977*, Jerusalem, Jerusalem Academic Press.

Ayalon, A. (1987) *Language and Change in the Arab Middle East*, Oxford, Oxford University Press.

Berelson, R., Lazarfeld, P. and McPhee, W. (1954) *Voting*, Chicago, University of Chicago Press.

Binder, L. (1988) *Islamic Liberalism*, Chicago, University of Chicago Press.

Birnbaum, P., Lively, J. and Parry, G. (eds) (1978) *Democracy, Consensus and Social Contract*, London, Sage.

Borthwick, B. M. (1980) *Comparative Politics of the Middle East*, New Jersey, Prentice Hall.

Bulloch, J. (1977) *Death of a Country*, London, Weidenfeld and Nicolson.

Cammack, P., Poole, D. and Tordoff, W. (1988) *Third World Politics*, London, Macmillan.

Chazan, N., Mortimer, R., Ravenhill, J. and Rothchild, D. (1988) *Politics and Society in Contemporary Africa*, Boulder, CO, Lynne Rienner.

Choudhury, G. W. (1990) *Islam and the Contemporary World*, London, Indus Thames.

Choueiri, Y. (1990) *Islamic Fundamentalism*, London, Pinter. Committee Against Repression and for Democratic Rights in Iraq (1991) *Saddam's Iraq*, London, Zed Press.

Clapham, C. (1985) *Third World Politics*, London, Croom Helm.

Cudsi, A. and Dessouki, A. (1981) *Islam and Power*, London, Croom Helm.

Dahl, R. (1956) *A Preface to Democratic Theory*, Chicago, University of Chicago Press.

Darwish, A. and Alexander, G. (1991) *Unholy Babylon*, London, V. Gollancz.

Deutsch, K. W. (1953) *Nationalism and Social Communication*, New York, John Wiley.
Diamond, L., Linz, J. and Lipset, S. M. (1989) *Democracy in Developing Countries, Vol. 3*, London, Adamantine Press.
Fisk, R. (1990) *Pity the Nation*, Oxford, Oxford University Press.
Ghods, R. (1990) *Iran in the 20th Century*, London, Adamantine Press.
Gilmour, D. (1983) *Lebanon, The Fractured Country*, London, Martin Robertson.
Gubser, P. (1973) *Politics and Change in Al-Karak, Jordan*, London, Croom Helm.
Halliday, F. and Alavi, H. (eds) (1988) *State and Ideology in the Middle East and Pakistan*, London, Macmillan.
Hudson, M. (1977) *Arab Politics*, New Haven, CT, Yale University Press.
ITN Factbook. (1990) London, M. O'Mara.
Ismael, T. Y. (1970) *Governments and Politics of the Contemporary Middle East*, Ontario, Pinter.
Joseph, R. (1987) *Democracy and Prebendal Politics in Nigeria. The Rise and Fall of the Second Republic*, Cambridge, Cambridge University Press.
Kariel, H. (ed.) (1970) *Frontiers of Democratic Theory*, New York, Syracuse University Press.
Kelly, J. (1980) *Arabia, the Gulf and the West*, London, Weidenfeld and Nicolson.
Khadduri, M. (1978) *Socialist Iraq*, Washington, DC, Middle East Institute.
Khouri, F. J. (1977) *The Arab Israeli Dilemma*, New York, Syracuse University Press.
Kornhauser, W. (1957) *The Politics of Mass Society*, New York, Free Press.
Lauterpacht, E., Greenwood, C. B., Weller, M. and Bethlehem, D. (eds) (1991) *The Kuwait Crisis: Basic Documents*. Cambridge International Documents Series, Vol. 1, Cambridge, Cambridge University Press.
Lerner, D. (1958) *The Passing of Traditional Society*, Glencoe, Free Press.
Lijphart, A. (1977) *Democracy in Plural Societies – A Comparative Exploration*, New Haven, CT, Yale University Press.
Lipset, S. M. (1966) *Political Man*, London, Heinemann Education.
Luciani, G. (1990) *The Arab State*, London, Routledge.
Macpherson, C. B. (1973) *Democratic Theory – Essays in Retrieval*, Oxford, Oxford University Press.
Matar, F. (1981) *Saddam Hussein The Man, The Cause and The Future*, London, Third World Centre.
Ma'oz, M. and Yaniv, A. (1986) *Syria Under Assad*, London, Croom Helm.
Maull, H. and Pick, O. (eds) (1989) *The Gulf War*, London, Pinter.
Middle East and North Africa (1990) London, Europa.
Mill, J. S. (n.d.) *Considerations of Representative Government*, London. Original publication.
Morris, B. (1987) *The Birth of the Palestinian Refugee Problem 1947–1949*, Cambridge, Cambridge University Press.
Mostyn, T. (1991) *Iran, Iraq and the Arabian Peninsular 1945–1990*, London, Facts on File.
Muravchik, J. (1991) *Exporting Democracy*, Washington, DC, American Enterprise Institute.
Owen, R. (1992) *State Power and Politics in the Making of the Modern Middle East*, London, Routledge.
Pennock, J. R. (ed.) (1964) *Self-government in Modernising Nations*, New Jersey, Prentice Hall.
Peretz, D. (1983) *The Middle East Today*, New York, Praeger.
Piscatori, J. (1986) *Islam in a World of Nation States*, Cambridge, Cambridge University Press.
Piscatori, J. (1991) *Islamic Fundamentalism and the Gulf Crisis*, Chicago, Cambridge University Press.

Political Report of the 8th congress of the Arab Ba'ath Socialist Party in Iraq, January 1974. London (1979).
Pridham, B. R. (ed.) (1985) *The Arab Gulf and the West*, London, Croom Helm.
Pye, L. (ed.) (1963) *Communications and Poltical Development*, Princeton, NJ, Princeton University Press.
Randall, V. (ed.) (1988) *Political Parties in the Third World*, London, Sage.
Randall, V. and Theobalds, R. (1985) *Political Change and Underdevelopment: A Critical Introduction to Third World Politics*, London, Macmillan.
Schlaim, A. (1990) *The Politics of Partition*, London, Oxford University Press.
Schumpeter, J. (1957) *Capitalism, Socialism and Democracy*, London, Allen and Unwin.
Seale, P. (1965) *The Struggle for Syria*, London, Oxford University Press.
Seale, P. (1990) *Assad*, London, Tauris.
Silberstein, L. (ed.) (1991) *New Perspectives on Israeli History*, New York, New York University Press.
Sluglett, M. F. and Sluglett, P. (1990) *Iraq since 1958*, London, I.B. Taurus.
Tahir-Kheli, S. and Ayubi, S. (eds) (1983) *Iran/Iraq War: New Weapons Old Conflicts*, New York, Praeger.
Toynbee, A. (1953) *The World and the West*, London, Oxford University Press.
VanDam, N. (1979) *The Struggle for Power in Syria*, London, Croom Helm.
Ward, R. and Rustow, D. (eds) (1964) *Political Modernisation in Japan and Turkey*, Princeton, NJ, Princeton University Press.
Welch, C. (ed.) (1967) *Political Modernisation*, Belmont, Wadsworth Pub. Co.
Wilson, M. (1987) *King Abdullah, Britain and the Making of Jordan*, London, Cambridge University Press.
Wright, M. (ed.) (1989) *Iran, The Khomeini Revolution*, London, Longman.

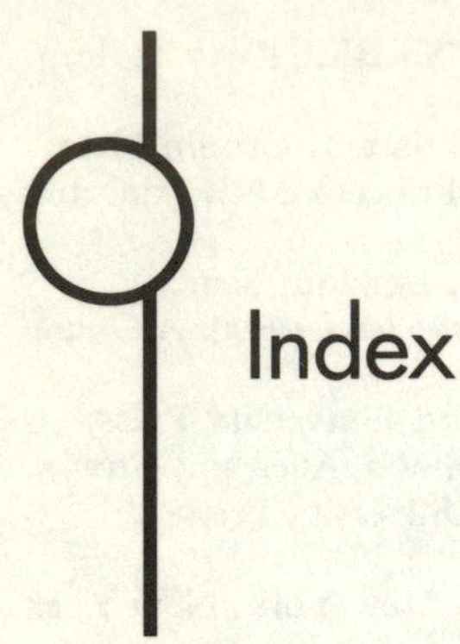

Index